£16.50

English for the utomobile Industry

EXPRESS SERIES

Marie Kavanagh

D1423524

OXFORD

OXFORD
UNIVERSITY PRESS

Great Clarendon Street, Oxford OX2 6DP

Oxford University Press is a department of the University of Oxford.
It furthers the University's objective of excellence in research,
scholarship,
and education by publishing worldwide in

Oxford New York

Auckland Cape Town Dar es Salaam Hong Kong Karachi
Kuala Lumpur Madrid Melbourne Mexico City Nairobi
New Delhi Shanghai Taipei Toronto

With offices in

Argentina Austria Brazil Chile Czech Republic France Greece
Guatemala Hungary Italy Japan Poland Portugal Singapore
South Korea Switzerland Thailand Turkey Ukraine Vietnam

OXFORD and OXFORD ENGLISH are registered trade marks of
Oxford University Press in the UK and in certain other countries

© Oxford University Press 2007

The moral rights of the author have been asserted

Database right Oxford University Press (maker)

First published 2007

2011 2010 2009 2008 2007

10 9 8 7 6 5 4 3 2 1

ISBN-13: 978 0 19 457901 8

Typeset by Oxford University Press
in Meta

Printed in Spain by Just Colour Graphic, S.L.

ACKNOWLEDGEMENTS

Illustrations by: Barking Dog Art pp 11a, 026a, 027a, 038b, 038c, 038d,
042a, 053a, 055a; Debbie Kelsey pp 012g, 013a, 020a, 027b, 029a,
029b, 029c, 033a, 047a, 063a ,064a

*The publishers would like to thank the following for their kind permission to
reproduce photographs and other copyright material*: Alamy Images pp 34,
49; Aluminium Federation p 41, BMW pp 7d, 7i, 12d, 12e, 25b, 48d,
50; Birgit Havenith and Nicole Rubba at Daimler Chrysler pp 7b, 7f,
12d, 19, 38, 40, 48a, 59; Ford pp 07a, 7e, 07f, 7g, 07j, 07k, 8a, 014d,
014f, 043a, 047a; Fotolia pp 7c, 14a, 14f, 16, 56, 57c, 61; Getty Images
p 22, Oxford University Press Classet pp 5, 17, 28, 43b; Porsche pp
12b, 12f, 48c; Volkswagen pp 12c, 12e, 48b, 57b, 57d

Cover images courtesy of: Getty Images (main image/Barry Willis/Taxi;
bottom left/Bruno Vincent/Reportage), Punchstock (top left/Image
Source).

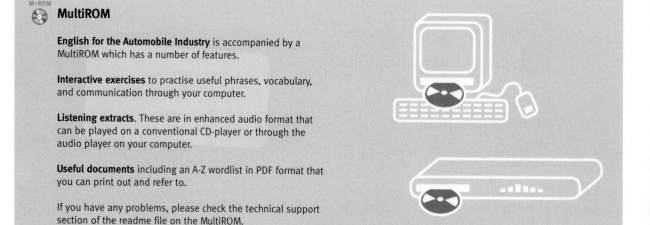

M-ROM

💿 MultiROM

English for the Automobile Industry is accompanied by a
MultiROM which has a number of features.

Interactive exercises to practise useful phrases, vocabulary,
and communication through your computer.

Listening extracts. These are in enhanced audio format that
can be played on a conventional CD-player or through the
audio player on your computer.

Useful documents including an A-Z wordlist in PDF format that
you can print out and refer to.

If you have any problems, please check the technical support
section of the readme file on the MultiROM.

Contents

About the book

English for the Automobile Industry has been developed specifically for people who work in the automobile industry who need English to communicate in a variety of situations with colleagues, clients, and business partners. It supplies you with the target vocabulary and commonly used expressions that are essential to communication whether you work directly for a car manufacturer, a supplier, in a car dealership, or for a marketing agency involved with the automobile industry.

English for the Automobile Industry covers a range of subjects to do with cars and the industry as a whole. Learners from purchasing or sales will find their needs catered for just as much as those from administration, design, or production. Units from the book work independently and can be selected according to the needs and interests of the course participants. **English for the Automobile Industry** is also ideal for self-study if learners feel they need to further their knowledge of the language specific to their industry.

The aim of all the units is to develop your communication skills. Each unit begins with a **Starter,** which consists of a short exercise or a quiz and serves as an introduction to the topic of the unit. Practical exercises, listening extracts, industry-specific texts as well as numerous photos and illustrations help you to acquire key vocabulary and expressions. Realistic role-plays give you the opportunity to put all you have learned into practice. Each unit closes with an **Output** activity, an article related to the topic of the unit followed by questions for reflection and discussion. Finally the book finishes up with a fun crossword to **Test yourself!** on all you have learned over the previous eight units.

The **MultiROM** contains all the **Listening extracts** from the book. These can be played through the audio player on your computer, or through a conventional CD-player. In order to give yourself extra listening practice, listen to it in your car. The **Interactive exercises** let you review your learning by doing **Useful phrases, Vocabulary, and Communication** exercises on your computer, this will be particularly valuable if you are using the book for self-study. There is also an **A-Z wordlist** with all the key words that appear in **English for the Automobile Industry**. This includes a column of phonetics and a space for you to write the translations of the words in your own language.

In the appendix of **English for the Automobile Industry** you will find the **Partner Files** for the role-plays, and the **Answer key** so that you can check your own answers if you are working alone. There are also **Transcripts** of the listening extracts, three pages of **Useful phrases and vocabulary**, and a **Weights and Measures Conversion Chart** which can be used as a handy reference at work.

1 Introduction to the car

STARTER

What words do you think of when you see a car? Complete the diagram below.

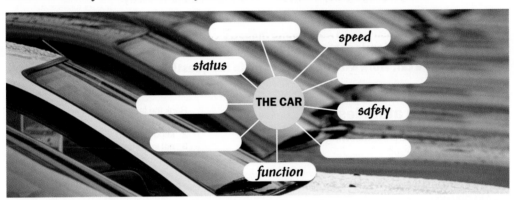

speed

status

THE CAR

safety

function

Now compare your diagram with others in your class.

AUDIO
2–5

1 **Different people have very different opinions about cars. Listen to the four speakers. Which person sees the car as:**

a   a status symbol?

b   a lifestyle product?

c   a functional product?

d   a danger to the environment?

Listen again and complete the sentences.

1   The _____ and the _____ features are very important. I put a lot of thought into the car I buy – it has to be me.

2   Of course if it's comfortable and safe, that's great, but I really don't care about the _____. I'm only interested in details such as the price, fuel consumption, how many seats there are, and how big the _____ is.

3   The car gives me prestige. I would only buy an expensive car with a powerful _____ and all the latest _____.

4   I live in the country and there's no public _____. But I think cars are polluting the world. Just think of all the _____ gases!

Who do you agree with most? Ask the other people in your class how they see their cars.
Use phrases from the box on page 6 to help you discuss. Do you have the same opinions?

2   Here are some of the factors people consider when buying a car.
Match the factors (1–7) to the definitions (a–g).

1	price	a	the amount of money you get when you sell your car
2	resale value	b	how much petrol or diesel the car uses
3	size	c	when customers always buy their cars from the same manufacturer
4	interior features	d	the amount of money you pay when you buy a car
5	fuel consumption	e	the car's capacity to go fast and accelerate quickly
6	performance	f	how big the car is
7	brand loyalty	g	items inside the car

3   The questionnaire below is part of a survey to find out which factors are important to people when they buy a car. Work with a partner to fill in the questionnaire.

Car buying attitudes

How important are the following factors
when buying a car?

Rank the factors like this:
1 very important
2 important
3 not important

Factors involved in buying a car	Your ranking	Partner's ranking
Price		
Resale value		
Design		
Colour		
Size		
Interior features		
Engine		
Fuel consumption		
Handling		
Brand name		
Brand loyalty		
Advertising		

Compare your results with others in the class. What are the five most important factors?

OPINIONS AND AGREEING OR DISAGREEING			
Asking for opinions	**Giving your opinion**	**Agreeing**	**Disagreeing**
What do you think?	I think …	I agree.	No, sorry, I disagree.
How do you feel about this?	In my opinion …	I think so too.	I'm afraid I don't agree.
What's your opinion of … ?	If you ask me …	Yes, that's right.	I can't go along with that.

4 **Work with a partner to label the types of cars.**

> convertible • ~~coupe~~ • estate (car) • hatchback • pick up • saloon •
> sports car • limousine • SUV

a

coupe

b

c

d

e

f

g

h

i

British English	American English
estate car	station wagon
saloon	sedan
camper van	recreational vehicle (RV)

Find the cars which fit the descriptions.

Which car(s) ...

1 has/have lots of room for passengers?
2 is/are good for driving on bad roads?
3 is/are not suitable for large families?
4 is/are perfect for hot, sunny weather?

5 has/have low fuel consumption?
6 is/are ideal for small parking spaces?
7 has/have only one passenger seat?
8 is/are good for transporting things?

AUDIO
6

5 Your son has just passed his driving test and you are going to buy him his first car. What questions would you ask a salesman before buying the car? Listen to the dialogue between John and Alison, and a salesman. Did they ask the same questions as you?

Listen again and complete the table of standard features with no extra cost.

Driver airbag	Yes/No
Passenger airbag	Yes/No
Lateral airbags	Yes/No
ABS	Yes/No
No. of cylinders	
mpg	
Top speed	
CD-autochanger	Yes/No
Satellite navigation	Yes/No
Sports steering wheel	Yes/No
Leather seats	Yes/No

British English	American English
engine	(also) motor
petrol	gas(oline)

6 Now match words from the two boxes to form expressions from the dialogue.

1	crash	5	brand
2	standard	6	resale
3	fuel	7	leather
4	diesel	8	passenger

a	consumption	e	seats
b	tests	f	image
c	value	g	airbags
d	equipment	h	engine

Complete the sentences using the expressions on page 8.

1   Taking good care of your car can increase its _resale value_ .

2   A high quality CD player comes as _____ with this model.

3   I drive a car with a _____ because of the better fuel consumption.

4   Manufacturers use _____ to improve the safety of their cars.

5   Volkswagen improved Skoda's _____ after it took over the company.

6   This model has a _____ of 3.3 litres per 100 km.

7   _____ are standard equipment throughout Europe.

8   This model has optional _____ with black headrests.

7   **Which cars would you recommend for the people below? Compare your choices with a partner.**

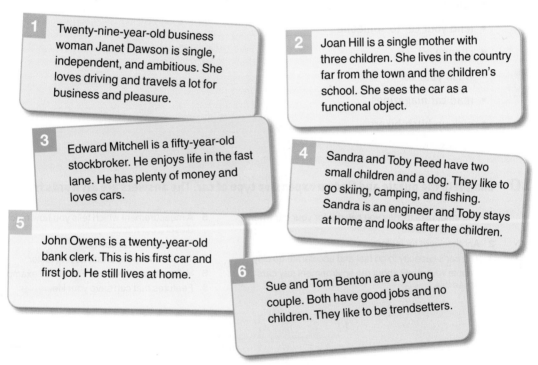

1   Twenty-nine-year-old business woman Janet Dawson is single, independent, and ambitious. She loves driving and travels a lot for business and pleasure.

2   Joan Hill is a single mother with three children. She lives in the country far from the town and the children's school. She sees the car as a functional object.

3   Edward Mitchell is a fifty-year-old stockbroker. He enjoys life in the fast lane. He has plenty of money and loves cars.

4   Sandra and Toby Reed have two small children and a dog. They like to go skiing, camping, and fishing. Sandra is an engineer and Toby stays at home and looks after the children.

5   John Owens is a twenty-year-old bank clerk. This is his first car and first job. He still lives at home.

6   Sue and Tom Benton are a young couple. Both have good jobs and no children. They like to be trendsetters.

8   **Work together with a partner to do the following role-play.**

Partner A: You want to buy a new car for yourself. Tell the salesperson what your requirements are.
Partner B: You are the salesperson in the car showroom. Help the customer.

RECOMMENDING	
I recommend ...	If I were you, I would buy a ...
You need a car which ...	A ... would be ideal/perfect for you.
Have you thought about ... ?	You should/shouldn't buy a ...
Why don't you buy a ... ?	

9 How well do you know your neighbour? Use words from the box to complete the table for you and your partner. Then work together to check your answers.

always • normally • frequently • often • sometimes • seldom • never

How often do you ... ?	You	Your neighbour
• buy a new car		
• check your tyre pressure		
• travel on holiday by car		
• tow a caravan		
• go over the speed limit		
• hire a car		
• lend your car to someone		
• change oil		
• wash your car		
• read car magazines		
• pick up hitch-hikers		

10 Complete the puzzle and find an expensive type of car. The answers are all words from this unit.

1 The amount of money you can get for your car when you want to sell it.

2 Another word for motor.

3 The car's capacity to go fast and accelerate quickly.

4 People who worry about the environment say cars cause this.

5 A measurement which tells you how much petrol or diesel a car needs.

6 The fastest a car can go.

7 This is a very important buying factor.

8 Volkswagen, Opel, and Fiat are all examples of this.

9 Features that can save your life.

Read the magazine article and answer the questions which follow.

What's in a name?

Have you ever thought about car names? Do they actually mean anything? And do you know what the name of *your* car means?

For example, you may think 'Rover' is just a name, but there is never *just* a name in marketing. A rover is a wanderer – someone who likes to travel around. So the name suggests mobility, freedom, having fun, and going wherever you want to go. These were important qualities when Rover cars first came on the market.

Marketing departments of car companies spend a lot of time and money thinking up names for cars. The names should be a reflection of the brand, product, and target group. The car you drive tells the world about your status, how much money you have, and the socio-economic group you belong to (or want to belong to). Good car names are catchy and fit the product, such as the 'Beetle' or the 'Mini'.

The name should also appeal to a global audience. At the very least, the name should not mean anything bad in another language. (This was why Rolls-Royce decided not to use the name 'Silver Mist' for one model: mist means animal manure in German!)

American car makers like to give their SUVs names that remind people of the Wild West, full of adventure and danger. Did you know that 'Wrangler' is another word for cowboy? Or that 'Maverick' means an unbranded cow that has strayed from the herd? People who own SUVs seldom drive them off-road, but they enjoy the feeling of excitement that the name creates.

OVER TO YOU

How important is the name of a car to you? Would you buy a car even if you didn't like the name? How many car names do you know the meaning of?

Imagine you work in the marketing department of a large car maker and you want to produce a small sports car with women as a target group. What would you call it?

2 The exterior

It is important for car makers that customers can easily identify the front and the rear of their cars. How many of the cars below can you identify?

1 Label the parts of the car.

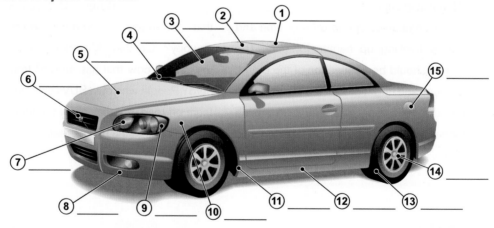

bonnet • front bumper • headlight • indicator • logo • petrol cap or flap • roof • sill • sunroof • tyre • wheel arch • wheel trim • windscreen • windscreen wiper • wing

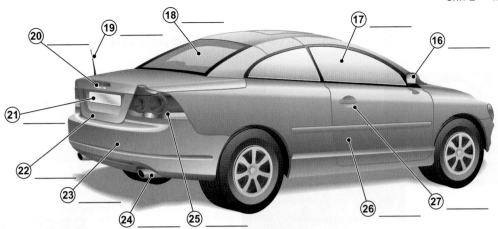

aerial • badge • boot • door •
door handle • exhaust pipe •
number plate • rear bumper • rear
window • wing mirror • side window
• rear light

British English	American English
aerial	antenna
bonnet	hood
boot	trunk
indicator	turn signal
number plate	license plate
petrol cap or flap	gas tank lid
tyre	tire
windscreen	windshield
wing	fender

2 **Complete the sentences using words from exercise 1.**

1 You open the _____*bonnet*_____ to look at the engine.

2 The _____ absorb small impacts in an accident.

3 Don't forget to retract the _____ before using the car wash.

4 Can you put my suitcases in the _____, please?

5 When it starts raining, you need to switch on the _____.

6 'What model is that?' 'I don't know, I can't see the _____ from here.'

7 It is important to inflate the _____ to the correct pressure for better fuel consumption.

8 The Mercedes star is a well-known _____.

9 Open the _____ and let some sun and fresh air into the car.

10 I wish all drivers would use their _____ when they want to turn right or left!

3 **Match the words from the two boxes to find the exterior car parts.**

1	head	6	petrol
2	brake	7	windscreen
3	exhaust	8	side
4	wheel	9	door
5	front	10	number

wipers	cap
lights	mirror
plate	handle
trim	lights
bumper	pipe

AUDIO
7–11

4 Listen to the descriptions of different car parts. Match the pictures to the descriptions and say what they are called.

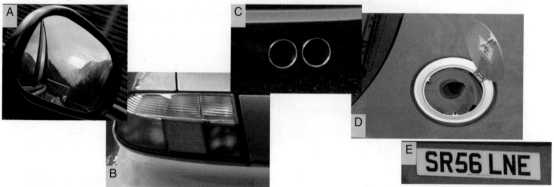

A

B

C

D

E SR56 LNE

Speaker: 1 [e] 2 ☐ 3 ☐ 4 ☐ 5 ☐

Now describe another car part in a similar way. Can the other students guess which car part you are describing?

5 Read the text about car production and complete the diagram on page 15.

BUILT TO ORDER

Almost every car is produced to the customer's specific requirements – a built-to-order car.

As soon as a car is ordered and a delivery date agreed, weekly and daily production schedules are created and sent to outside suppliers and the company's own pre-assembly stations. This is to make sure that all the necessary components arrive on time.

First of all, a small data carrier is attached to the floor pan in the body shop. This data carrier contains all the customer's specifications and communicates wirelessly with control units along the production line. In the body shop the floor pan, wheel arches, side panels, and roof are welded together by robots to make the frame of the car. The add-on parts – the doors, boot lid, and bonnet – are then mounted to make the body-in-white.

The finished body shell then goes into the paint shop where the data carrier determines the colour. In final assembly, the interior and exterior parts (for example the front and rear bumpers, headlights, windscreen, and other windows) are fitted. After quality control and a final check, the finished car can be released. It is now ready for delivery to its new owner.

1 Car is ordered and _delivery date_ ª agreed

2 _____ ᵇ are created and sent to suppliers and _____ ᶜ

3 _____ ᵈ containing specifications is attached to _____ ᵉ in body shop

4 Floor pan, _____ ᶠ, side panels, and _____ ᵍ are welded together

5 _____ ʰ are mounted

6 Body shell goes into _____ ⁱ

7 Interior and exterior parts are fitted in _____ ʲ

8 _____ ᵏ and a final check are done

9 _____ ˡ is released

THE PASSIVE

We often use the passive voice to describe a process. It is formed using the verb *to be* and the past participle (the 3rd form of the verb). We use *by* to say who or what does the action.

*Almost every car **is produced** to the customer's specifications.*
*The floor pan … and the roof **are welded by** robots.*
*The finished car **can be released**.*

---

6   Complete the sentences below using the passive form of the verbs in brackets.

1   This model ___*is produced*___ (produce) in the new factory in Poland.

2   German cars _____ (sell) all over the world.

3   The orders _____ (can/place) by fax or online.

4   The cars _____ (assemble) by robots.

5   Spare parts _____ (can/buy) from your local dealer.

6   The interiors _____ (design) by computer.

7   Tyres _____ (should/replace) before they wear down completely.

7   Look at the diagram in exercise 5 again. Work with a partner and describe the car production process in your own words. The phrases in the box will help you.

DESCRIBING A PROCESS

Firstly/The first step is/To begin with …	After that …	Finally …
Secondly …	Then …	The last step/stage is …
The next step/stage is …	Following that …	

8   **Look at these steps for changing a tyre and put them in the right order.**

Start like this: The first step is to put the vehicle into gear or park (e). Then you ...

a   Remove the old tyre from under the vehicle and lower the vehicle.

b   Take the spare tyre out of the boot and make sure it is in good condition.

c   Check again to make sure the wheel nuts are tight.

d   Remove the tyre and put it under the vehicle, next to the jack.

e   Put the vehicle into gear (manual transmission) or park (automatic).

f   Use a jack to raise the vehicle.

g   Fit the spare tyre and tighten the wheel nuts.

h   Find two rocks or large pieces of wood and put them in front of and behind the opposite wheel.

i   Loosen the wheel nuts slightly.

j   Loosen the wheel nuts more and remove them.

1 [e]   2 ☐   3 ☐   4 ☐   5 ☐
6 ☐   7 ☐   8 ☐   9 ☐   10 ☐

AUDIO

12

Now listen to the recording to check your answers.

9   **Work with a partner. Write a description of one of the processes below, using phrases from page 15, and a dictionary to help you. Then read your description to another pair. Can they add anything to your description?**

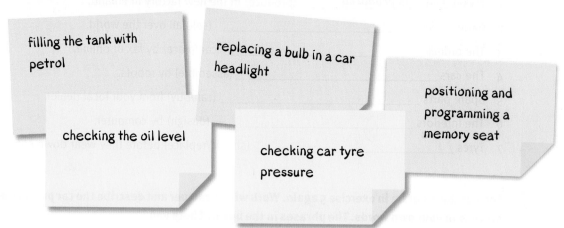

filling the tank with petrol

replacing a bulb in a car headlight

positioning and programming a memory seat

checking the oil level

checking car tyre pressure

10   **Discuss the following questions with a partner.**

What problems do you have to deal with in your job? How do you solve them?
What was the last problem you had to solve at work?
Do you ever have problems with suppliers?

11 **A manufacturer phones a supplier to complain about a problem with some headlights.**
Complete the dialogue by putting the manufacturer's lines into the right place.
What is the problem exactly? What do you think the cause of the problem could be?

Manufacturer

a I'm afraid there is. In our tests there's been a much higher failure rate than is allowed in the contract.

b Fine, thanks. Listen Alex, I'm calling about the headlights we received from you last week.

c It's around 5 per cent. And as you know, it should be under 1 per cent.

d That's really good of you, Alex. I'll be in my office until about 4 pm. After that you can reach me on my mobile.

e Hi, Alex. It's Chris Fraser here from Rover.

f Thanks, Alex. Speak to you later.

g Yes. It's 0044 795 4345381.

h Sure. It's A348.

i Yes, that's right.

Supplier

1 Halla Systems. Alex Newman speaking. ⟶ `e`

2 Ah, hi Chris. How's it going? ⟵

3 Uh huh. Is there a problem with the headlights?

4 Oh dear. I'm sorry to hear that. Can you tell me what the failure rate is exactly?

5 You're right, that's completely unacceptable. Could you just give me the consignment number, please?

6 Got you. OK Chris, this is what I'm going to do. I'll look into the problem straight away and will get back to you as soon as I can.

7 OK. I think I've got your mobile number, but can you give it to me again just in case?

8 Let me just read that back to you. 0044 795 4345381 – is that right?

9 Great. OK Chris, like I said, I'll call you as soon as I know something. Bye now.

AUDIO
13
Now listen to the recording to check your answers.

12 **Find phrases in the dialogue which mean the same as the phrases below.**

1 How are you?

2 The reason I am calling ...

3 Can I have it again ...

4 Can I just repeat that?

5 You can contact me later on ...

6 I'll ring you when I have more information.

7 We'll be in touch later.

13 When Alex looks into the problem, he discovers that the bulbs used in the headlights from consignment A348 came from a new supplier. Work with a partner to do two role-plays. The phrases in the box will help you.

PARTNER FILES   Partner A   File 1, p. 62
Partner B   File 12, p. 64

TELEPHONING PHRASES

This is ... from ...	I'm sorry, I didn't catch that.
I'm calling about ...	I'll call you back later.
Can I speak to ..., please?	I'll send you ... by fax/email.
Could you tell me the name of your company?	Just give me a call if you have any more problems.
Could you repeat that, please?	Thanks for calling.

---

14 8D reports are often used in the automobile industry to help solve quality problems.

a apply suitable oil

b sort out parts

c quality assurance for supplier parts

d squeaky noise when operating electrical window switch

e plastic rubbing on metal

f change surface roughness of parts

g watch for similar problem on all models

h no reoccurence predicted

8D Report		Customer:	
		Customer Ref:	
		Supplier Ref:	
		Date:	
To:	**Product:**		
1 Team responsible:			
2 Problem description:			
3 Containment action(s):	Person resp.:	% Effectiveness:	Date:
4 Root cause(s):		% Contribution:	
5 Selected long-term corrective action(s):		Review:	% Effectiveness:
6 Implemented long-term corrective action(s):		Date:	Person resp.:

7	Action to prevent reoccurrence of problem:		Date:	Person resp.:
8	Comments (Information to team):	Processed by:		
	Date of close:			

Now complete the 8D report, either for the problem you solved in the role-plays or for a problem you had in real life. Then show the 8D report to another student, and explain how you solved the problem.

OUTPUT

Read the magazine article and answer the questions.

The Smart

Mercedes-Benz and SMH, the Swiss producer of the Swatch, formed a joint-venture called Micro Compact car (MCC). MCC's goal was to produce a small two-seater called the Smart.

MCC and its main suppliers invested more than $1.15 billion in the Smart. It is built at a new factory called Smartville in eastern France. Each car takes only five hours to build. The car is just 2.5 metres long, 556 mm shorter than the original Mini and two-thirds the size of a conventional hatchback. The target group is mainly young urban dwellers because of its urban mobility and parkability.

The car is practical and versatile, as the Smart's body panels can be changed in under an hour. It is the only car on the market where buyers can change the colour and design so easily. The changeover costs between £450–700.

The original engine was a 3-cylinder petrol or diesel engine with 599cc and 54bhp. It had a top speed of 85 mph and an acceleration of 0–60 mph in 17 seconds. Since the first launch Smart has introduced derivatives such as a four-door version, a convertible, and other eingines to choose from.

All models have a 36-month or 25,000-mile warranty.

OVER TO YOU

Do you own a Smart or would you ever buy one?

What are the advantages and disadvantages of the Smart?

In which countries do you think small cars are most successful?

Do you think small cars will become more popular in the future? Why or why not?

3 The interior

STARTER

Find someone in your class who ...

- has a car with GPS navigation system
- likes to have lots of switches and gadgets in the car
- always buys a car with air conditioning
- has soft toys and cushions in the car

- needs plenty of legroom
- is a telematics user
- likes a sporty steering wheel
- doesn't allow smoking in his/her car

1 Label the parts of a car interior.

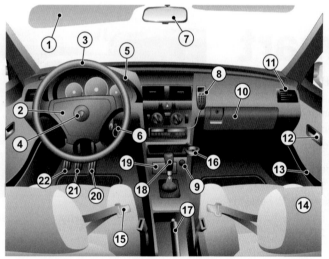

accelerator • air vent • airbag • ashtray • brake pedal • car seat (headrest) • cigarette lighter • clutch pedal • cup holder • dashboard • door handle • door tray • gearstick • glove compartment • handbrake • hands-free telephone • horn • ignition • rear-view mirror • seat belt • steering wheel • sun visor

1 _____
2 _____
3 _____
4 _____
5 _____
6 _____
7 _____

8 _____
9 _____
10 _____
11 _____
12 _____
13 _____
14 _____

15 _____
16 _____
17 _____
18 _____
19 _____
20 _____
21 _____
22 _____

British English	American English
accelerator	(also) gas pedal
gearstick	gear shift/stick shift
glove compartment	(also) glove box

2 **Complete the sentences using words from exercise 1.**

1 It's so practical to have a _____ near the steering wheel. I can take a drink whenever I want.

2 In a car with manual transmission, you need to press the _____ when you want to change gear.

3 There's usually a cosmetic mirror on the passenger's _____.

4 I have a leather _____. It's not so cold for my hands in the winter and it gives you a good grip.

5 It's against the law to phone while driving so I've ordered a car with a _____.

6 Could you have a look in the road atlas? It's in the _____.

7 I don't need a _____ as I don't smoke and I don't want anyone to smoke in my car.

8 Could you close the _____? I'm getting a draught.

3 **Match the numbers to the instruments.**

coolant temperature gauge ☐
driver information system ☐
engine oil temperature gauge ☐
warning/indicator lights ☐
fuel gauge ☐
rev counter ☐
speedometer ☐
voltmeter ☐

4 **Look at the picture and say which instrument ...**

1 shows you how fast the car is travelling?
2 warns you if the engine lubrication system gets too hot?
3 shows that you are indicating to turn left or right?
4 shows you how often the engine is turning over?
5 shows you how much petrol you have in the tank?
6 indicates the voltage of the car's electrical system?

5   **Work with a partner to do the following role-play.**

You are two managers from the marketing department. You are meeting to decide whether or not you should remove the cigarette lighter and ashtray as standard equipment. First look at the phrases in the box, then look at your role cards.

PARTNER FILES → Partner A   File 2, p. 62
Partner B   File 13, p. 64

SUGGESTIONS

Making suggestions	Accepting suggestions	Rejecting suggestions
Why don't we … ?	That sounds good.	I don't think that will work.
How about …ing … ?	I think that'll work.	That's (maybe) not (such) a good idea because …
I suggest …	Good idea.	I'm not sure about that.
We could …		

6   **What do you need to do when you first get into a car, before you start the engine?**
Continue the list on the note paper with a partner.

1) Adjust seat (if necessary)
2)
3)

AUDIO
14

7   **Listen to and complete the following dialogue between a driving instructor and a learner taking a first driving lesson.**

Instructor   OK, so you're sitting in the car. What do you do now?
Learner   Well, I start the car. No, wait! I check behind me first before I drive away.
Instructor   You've forgotten something.
Learner   Of course, I fasten my _____ [1] first.
Instructor   Even before you fasten your seat belt there are things you need to do. First of all, are you sitting comfortably?
Learner   Not really. The seat is a bit too far from the _____ [2].
Instructor   So you need to adjust the seat, right? Use the two levers there to adjust the position and the height. You can also adjust the steering wheel. So now you're sitting comfortably. What should you check now?
Learner   That the _____ [3] mirror is in the right position. And the side mirror.
Instructor   Quite right. What next?
Learner   Well, if it's dark, I need to switch on the _____ [4].
Instructor   Good. Finally, before you put the key into the _____ [5], what should you do?
Learner   Now I fasten my seat belt.

Did your list in 6 match the instructions from the instructor?

8 Cover the dialogue on page 22. Can you remember which nouns can follow which verbs? Complete the table. When you have finished, check your answers on page 22.

> ~~bonnet~~ • boot • door • ~~fog lights~~ • fuel • glove compartment • headlights • headrest • indicator • ~~oil level~~ • petrol cap • ~~rear-view mirrow~~ • seat belt • seat height • seat position • side mirror • steering wheel • sunroof • tyre pressure • windscreen wipers

Open/Close	Adjust	Switch on/off	Check
bonnet	*rear-view mirror*	*fog lights*	*oil level*

9 Now work with a partner to answer the following questions. Using phrases from the table above.

What do you do when ...

1 visibility is poor because of fog? _____

2 your seat is too low? _____

3 you think you need oil? _____

4 you want to get out of the car? _____

5 you can't see the cars behind you properly? _____

6 it's getting dark? _____

7 you want to look at the engine? _____

8 your steering wheel is too high? _____

9 you think your tyre pressure is low? _____

10 you need your road map? _____

11 it's warm and sunny? _____

12 your passenger has no legroom in the back? _____

_____

10 You work for a German company that manufactures car parts. You receive the email below from a French customer. Complete the email using the words in the box.

> appreciate • attachment • forward • possible • sending • unfortunately • writing

---

Untitled Message

File Edit View Insert Format Tools Table Window Help

Send

To...

Cc...

Subject: order no. 7H325K

From: Perry, Yves <yperry@sr-g.fr>

Dear ...

I'm _____ ¹ to you because of a problem with the delivery which we received from you last week. The order was for 1000 dashboard panels. _____ ² 50 of the boxes that arrived were empty. Can you send us the missing items as soon as _____ ³? We would also _____ ⁴ it if you could look into the problem to make sure this does not happen again. I'm _____ ⁵ you a scan of the delivery note as an _____ ⁶ .

I look _____ ⁷ to hearing from you soon.

Best regards
Yves Perry

Now write a reply to the email. The phrases in the box will help you.

EMAIL PHRASES	
Thank you for your email.	I'm sending you ...
I'm writing to ...	I hope that ...
I'm very sorry about ...	Let me know if ...
Could you ... ?	Best regards/Best wishes

11   Many car manufacturers now have car 'configurators' on their websites. These allow customers to design their cars online before they buy. Look at the configurator and match the menu titles (a–f) to the menus (1–6).

a   Audio/Communication
b   Safety/Technology
c   Exterior equipment
d   Seats
e   Interior equipment
f   Wheels/Tyres

Home   /   **New Cars**   /   Used Cars   /   Customer Service   /   Financial Services   /   Car Accessories

CAR CONFIGURATOR: CHOOSE YOUR EQUIPMENT

1	2	3	4	5	6
☐ Electric adjustable and heated door mirrors, with memory ☐ Remote control central locking ☐ Electric slide and tilt glass sunroof ☐ Towing equipment (removable)	☐ Electronic tyre pressure monitoring ☐ 8J x 17 'seven spoke' design alloy wheels with 235/55 R17 tyres ☐ 8.5J x 19 'twelve spoke' design alloy wheels with 255/40 R19 tyres	☐ Electronic climate control with individual driver and front passenger controls ☐ Garage door opener ☐ Rear window blind, electrically operated ☐ Interior light pack	☐ Electric front seats – 14 way adjustable, with memory for front seats ☐ Leather upholstery ☐ Heated front and rear seats ☐ Sports seats	☐ Anti-theft alarm with tow-away protection ☐ Cruise control ☐ Xenon headlights ☐ Adaptive air suspension	☐ DVD-based navigation system ☐ Hands-free dual-band/GSM car telephone ☐ Voice control system ☐ Active speakers

Which of the menus would the following items belong to?

A   Driver and front passenger two-stage airbags
B   Child seat mounting system
C   CD autochanger for 6 discs
D   255/45 R18 low profile tyres
E   Deluxe front centre armrest
F   Headlight cleaning system

12 Complete the puzzle. The answers are all words from this unit.

Across

1 You put your cigarette here when it's finished.

3 The instruments are on this.

5 This is the middle pedal in a car.

8 This stops the sun from shining into your eyes. (2 words)

9 You use this to change gear.

Down

2 This protects your head and neck in an accident.

4 You operate this when you park your car to stop it from moving.

6 You can put your maps and documents in this: … compartment

7 You look in this to check the traffic behind you: rear-view …

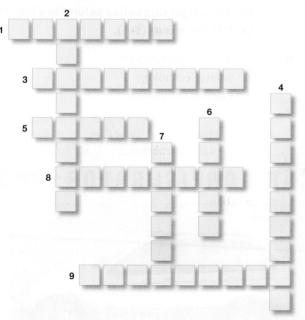

OUTPUT

Read the magazine article and answer the questions which follow.

Navigation aids, telematics equipment, audio system features, and the standard instruments are all fighting for space on the instrument panel (IP). This creates a challenge for interior designers and engineers who need to keep the IP simple so that the driver is not distracted by too many buttons and instruments. Customers also equate a spacious interior with luxury – another reason why the IP shouldn't look overcrowded.

Designers deal with the problem in various ways. They reduce the size of 'space-eaters' such as heating and cooling systems, or even remove them completely from the IP by putting them under the seat or in the boot. They also put many functions, such as station pre-set buttons for audio systems, on touch screens. Touch screens save space on the IP but there is still the danger of overcrowding the screen, which could distract the driver and thus cause an accident. Another problem is the position: the touch screen needs to be located high on the dashboard so that the driver can use it easily while driving. But if it is too high it can be hard to read because of reflections and the sun 'washing out' the screen.

Some engineers see voice recognition as a way to get rid of many manual controls and to simplify the IP. But voice recognition can also be overused. There needs to be an optimal balance between visual displays and voice instructions, so that the driver can deal safely with all the information he or she receives.

OVER TO YOU

Is the IP of your car user-friendly? Why or why not?

Which do you prefer – an IP that looks like a cockpit with lots of switches and controls, or a more simplified version?

How do you feel about voice recognition controls?

4 Under the bonnet

What do these abbreviations means? Work with a partner to see how many you know.

1 FWD   _front-wheel drive_

2 bhp   _____

3 g/km _____

4 GDI   _____

5 mpg   _____

6 mph   _____

7 Nm   _____

8 rpm   _____

9 RWD   _____

10 SI   _____

11 TDI   _____

I have a new car. It's FWD, TDI, and it's got ABS, CATS, ESP, ACC, ASR, and PAS

1 Label the diagram with the words below.

clutch • crankshaft • engine • gearbox • piston • propeller shaft

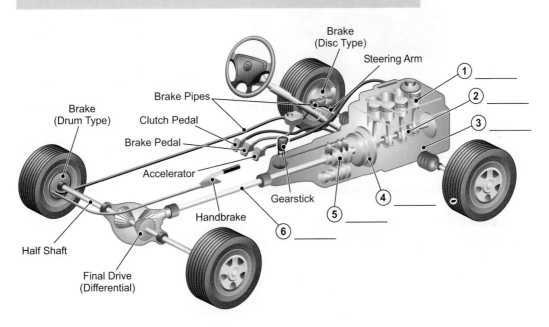

2   **Look at this extract from a tour of a car factory and complete the text with the words below.**

clutch • combustion • crankshaft • cylinders • distribution • fuel • piston • spark plug • torque

'Now we come to the engine. The principle of the internal _____ [1] engine has not changed in the last 100 years. The engine takes in _____ [2] and air which is compressed in a combustion chamber. Then this mixture is ignited by a _____ [3] to produce an explosion, which moves the _____ [4] in the cylinder. The up and down motion of the piston in the cylinder is converted into rotational motion by the _____ [5]. The rotational force generated by the engine is known as _____ [6].

The size of the engine determines the power. The more _____ [7] there are, the more powerful the engine. This power is transmitted through the _____ [8], the gearbox, the propeller shaft (in rear-wheel and four-wheel drive), and the axles to the wheels. The position of the engine can vary, but generally speaking it is mounted at the front. In some sports cars, the engine is mounted at the rear (eg, Porsche) or in the middle (eg, Ferrari or Lamborghini) because of weight _____ [9].

So, that's enough about the engine for the moment – let's move on to the next stage … '

AUDIO
15

Now listen to the recording to check your answers.

British English	American English
gearbox	transmission

3 Find words in exercise 2 and use your dictionary (if necessary) to complete the following table.

Verb	Noun	Adjective
to _____ a	power	_____ b
	_____ c	combustible
to _____ d	ignition	
to _____ e	_____ f	explosive
to _____ g	rotation	_____ h
to _____ i	transmission	

Now complete the sentences with the correct form of the words from the table.

1 In an engine, linear motion is converted into _____ motion by the crankshaft.

2 The power of the engine is _____ through the clutch and the gearbox.

3 The spark plug _____ the air/fuel mixture and sets off an _____.

4 A 6-cylinder engine is more _____ than a 4-cylinder engine.

5 Fuel and air is compressed in the _____ chamber.

4 Match the descriptions of engine layout to the diagrams.

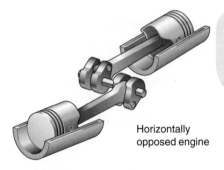

Horizontally
opposed engine

1 This layout is used for high performance engines with a compact layout such as in the BMW 7-series. The cylinders are arranged in two banks set at an angle to one another. This layout is normally more cubical in shape than the other two.

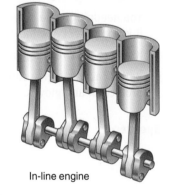

In-line engine

2 This layout is wide and flat and gives the engine a low centre of gravity. The cylinders are arranged in two banks on opposite sides of the engine. It is very practical for cars which have the engine located at the rear, such as Porsche.

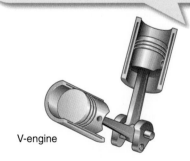

V-engine

3 This layout is long and narrow. The cylinders are all next to each other in a single bank. It is a standard, simple layout used in the Mercedes A-class, for example.

5   Work with a partner. First look at the phrases used to describe position and shape.
Then look at the engine layouts in your files. Tell your partner where the components from the
box below are.

battery • brake fluid reservoir • engine oil dipstick •
engine oil filler cap • power steering reservoir • radiator expansion
tank • windscreen/headlight washer container

PARTNER FILES ➤ Partner A   File 7, p. 63
Partner B   File 14, p. 64

DESCRIBING POSITION AND SHAPE

The ... is **on the right/left-hand side**
of the engine.
This part is located **at the front/rear**
of the engine.
It's **on the opposite side** of the engine
from the ...
It's **above/below/next to/beside** the ...
It's **between** the ... and the ...

This layout is **cubical** in
shape.
The brake fluid reservoir
is the **rectangular**
container on the right.

▢ square	⬛ cubical
▭ rectangular	⬭ cylindrical
● circular	● spherical
△ triangular	△ conical

AUDIO 16–23

6   Listen to seven questions from customers and match them to the answers given by a technical
support hotline employee.

a   You look at the level in the reservoir.

b   The cooling system is filled once at the factory and never has to be changed.

c   Oil consumption can be up to 1.0 l/1000 km so the engine oil level must be checked at regular
intervals. It is a good idea to check the oil level every time you put fuel in the car.

d   Under normal conditions you don't have to do anything with the battery except check the
electrolyte level occasionally.

e   You needn't go to a service station for a brake fluid change, but make sure the person who does
it is competent and has the necessary tools.

f   It's the plastic rectangular container next to the power steering reservoir.

g   Battery acid is highly corrosive so you mustn't work on the battery without wearing eye
protection and gloves.

Speaker: 1 ☑ *f*   2 ☐   3 ☐   4 ☐   5 ☐   6 ☐   7 ☐

AUDIO
23

7 A potential customer is visiting the stand of a major car manufacturer
at an international car show.

Listen to the dialogue and put these key
features in the order in which they are
mentioned.

a   low fuel consumption
b   design
c   top speed
d   six-speed automatic gearbox as standard
e   optional extras included in the price
f   acceleration from 0–60 in 6 seconds
g   increased power of the engine.

1 $\boxed{b}$ 2 ☐   3 ☐   4 ☐
5 ☐   6 ☐   7 ☐

Now listen again and note down what the numbers refer to.

1   4.2 _____

2   330 _____

3   155 _____

4   W12 and V6 _____

5   16.1 _____

6   23 _____

7   54,000 _____

8   18 _____

Discuss the questions with a partner.

1   Why does the visitor first look at the car?
2   Why does the car have low fuel consumption?
3   What two things does the rep give the visitor, and why?

8 Match the two parts of the sentences from the dialogue (listen again if necessary).

1   we have increased the power   a   an effect on fuel consumption.
2   a six-speed automatic gearbox   b   with a 3.7 and a 4.2-litre petrol engine.
3   We're launching the model   c   is a six-disc CD unit with nine speakers …
4   That naturally has   d   by 20 bhp to 330 bhp.
5   Included in the price   e   then just call or email me.
6   If you have any other questions,   f   comes as standard.

9 **Work with a partner to do the following role-play. First look at the box for phrases you can use. Then look at your role cards in the Partner Files.**

PARTNER FILES ➤ Partner A File 3, p. 62
Partner B File 15, p. 64

AT A TRADE FAIR

Visitor	**Sales rep**
I'd like more information on …	Can I help you?
I'm interested in …	Which car are you interested in?
What about … ?	Would you like more detailed information?
Can I take one of these brochures?	Would you like a brochure?
Could you tell me something about … ?	Here is our price list.
	Let me give you my (business) card.

10 **Complete this puzzle with words from the unit.**

Across

1 This keeps the brake lubricated: brake … .
3 This can be petrol or diesel.
5 This fluid is put in the cooling system.
7 The motion of the pistons rotate this.
10 You use a dipstick to check the … level.
11 You need electricity from this to start the engine.

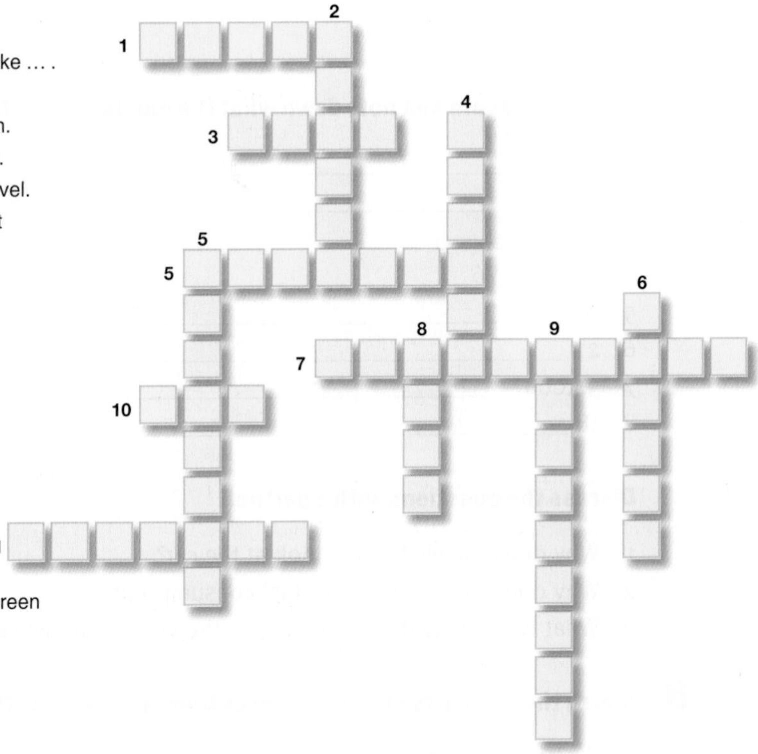

Down

2 A type of fuel.
4 This moves up and down in the cylinder.
5 A six-… engine.
6 This fluid is used to keep the windscreen clean: windscreen … .
8 This is highly corrosive: battery … .
9 This ignites the fuel-air mixture in petrol engines. (2 words)

Read the article and answer the questions which follow.

GDI Engines

When developing a new motor-vehicle engine, engineers are faced with the dilemma of more power or less fuel. The goal is to combine high power output and low fuel consumption. Increasing fuel efficiency helps motorists to save money and also reduces CO_2 emissions. Gasoline Direct Injection (GDI) engines can reduce fuel consumption by up to 20%, thereby producing 20% lower emissions.

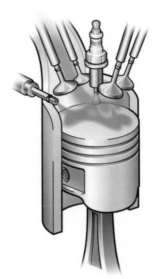

How does it work?

GDI engines use a new combustion control method that injects gasoline directly into the cylinders, where it mixes with oxygen from air drawn in from the outside. Conventional spark-ignition engines mix air and gasoline in the intake manifold before injecting the mixture into the cylinder.

The GDI engine produces a finer mist of gasoline in the cylinder which leads to cleaner burning and more power. It also has a shaped piston crown to swirl the finely atomized gasoline into a tight cloud near the tip of the spark plug. This stratified charge of fuel and fresh air near the source of ignition is the process behind GDI's low fuel consumption.

Some car makers have developed other key components, for example a high-pressure common-rail injection system with a single piston injection pump. This pump supplies the exact amount of fuel needed to maintain the required pressure in the system.

GDI engines will become more important in the future because of the need to reduce fuel consumption and because of growing environmental concerns.

OVER TO YOU

Can you explain in your own words how GDI engines work?

How important do you think GDI engines will be in the future?

Do you know of any other current engine innovations?

Performance and technical specifications

STARTER

Read these short descriptions of well-known cars. Can you guess which cars they are?

1 Two-door, mid-engined, four-wheel-drive sports car. The engine is 6.2-litre V12, with 571 bhp. The acceleration is 0–60 mph in 3.8 seconds with a top speed of 205 mph. The doors do not open conventionally.

2 The original model came on the market forty years ago and became an icon of 1960s Britain. The car became very famous in the film *The Italian Job*. The new version has a 163 bhp, inter-cooled 1.6-litre engine and a six-speed manual gearbox.

3 A four-door executive luxury saloon which has been completely updated and now has no gearstick and no handbrake but a large aluminium knob on the centre console. Most of the technical systems are operated by a 'controller' which acts like a computer mouse, or by up to 270 voice-activated commands.

Now think of a car yourself. Write a description and see if the others in your class can guess what it is.

AUDIO
1
24

A spokesperson for a major car maker is giving a presentation about a new car model and a journalist is asking questions. Listen to the recording, which features are not mentioned?

a running costs

b top speed

c front suspension

d body strength

e boot capacity

f start-stop automatic

g light-weight materials

h disc brakes

i new design

j chassis length

k fuel consumption

Listen to the recording again and complete the sentences from the dialogue below with the features above.

1 The _____ has been stiffened to produce more precise steering at high speeds.

2 We have also increased the size of the _____ for a shorter braking distance.

3 I also noticed that the press release says there is improved _____.

4 Firstly, we have enhanced the Cd value with a _____.

5 We have also reduced the kerb weight of the car by over 50 kilos by using _____.

6 We have introduced a _____ so that the engine cuts out if you stand still for more than three seconds and starts again when you take your foot off the brake.

7 This has a positive effect on the
   _____ of this car and, of course, on
   the resale value.
8 We have also increased the _____
   to make the car more practical for families and
   sports people.

Are the following sentences about the new XPT true or false?

1 Changes to the front suspension mean better steering when the car goes fast.
2 The car is now more expensive to run.
3 The car is not very economical for driving in town.
4 The interior and the boot are bigger than in the last model.

2 **Match the words from the two boxes to make expressions from the dialogue.**

1	urban	6	boot
2	Cd	7	front
3	running	8	disc
4	resale	9	kerb
5	braking		

costs	suspension
consumption	value
brakes	value
capacity	weight
distance	

Now match the expressions above with the correct definition.

a A measure of the car's wind resistance, or drag coefficient.
b The amount you spend on petrol, tax, maintenance, etc.
c The volume of the boot.
d How much fuel you need driving around town.
e Brake system which uses a calliper and rotor, or disc, to stop or slow a vehicle.
f How much you can expect to get if you sell the car after three years.
g The connection of the axles by springs and dampers to the car body which prevents occupants
   from feeling road shocks.
h The distance between putting your foot down on the brake and the car stopping.
i How much the car weighs when there are no passengers in it and with half a tank of fuel.

3 **Read the road tests for three cars and say which car ...**

a has the fastest acceleration from 0–60 mph?
b has the highest top speed?
c is the most expensive to buy?
d is the cheapest to run?

e has the best equipment?
f has the largest engine?
g has the most powerful engine?

Which car would you prefer to own?

		CAR 1	CAR 2	CAR 3
PERFORMANCE	0–60 mph (secs)	8.9	11.3	9.3
	0–100 mph (secs)	27.1	33.4	25.8
	Standing $\frac{1}{4}$ mile (secs/mph)	17.0/81.9	18.7/76.6	17.1/83.9
	Maximum speed (mph)	137	126	131
	30–70 mph thru gears	9.3	10.7	8.4
	Braking 70–0 mph (metres/feet)	47.03/154.3	47.06/154.4	47.6/156.2
COSTS	List price	£28,655	£29,085	£27,595
	Test/EU combined mpg	31.0/34.9	32.0/39.8	34.0/37.2
	Insurance group	14	13	13
	CO_2 (grammes per km)	219/29	180/21	197/D
EQUIPMENT	Airbags	4	4	4
	Alarm/immobiliser	yes/yes	yes/yes	yes/yes
	ABS/brake assist	yes/yes	yes/yes	yes/no
	Traction/ESP	ESP	ESP	TCS
	Climate control	yes	AC	yes
	Cruise control	yes	yes	yes
TECHNICAL	Engine/capacity	V6, 2496cc	4cyl, 16v, 2148cc	V6, 24v, 2962cc
	Maximum power	180bhp at 4,000rpm	143bhp at 4,200rpm	176bhp at 4,000rpm
	Maximum torque	273lb ft at 1,500rpm	232lb ft at 1,800rpm	257lb ft at 1,600rpm
	Transmission	six-speed manual	five-speed auto	five-speed manual
	Suspension (front)	ind four-link	ind double wishbone	ind Macpherson strut
	Suspension (rear)	double wishbone	multi-link, self-levelling	multi-link
	Brakes (front/rear)	ventilated disc/disc	ventilated disc/disc	ventilated disc/disc
	Tyres (front/rear)	235/45 R17	205/65 R15	225/45 R17
	Dimensions L/W (cm)	480/181	484/180	482/204
	Boot space (litres)	455/159	600/1,975	416/1,490
RESULT	Styling	● ● ● ●	● ●	● ● ● ●
	Performance	● ● ● ●	● ●	● ● ● ●
	Ride and handling	● ● ●	● ●	● ● ●
	Accommodation	● ● ● ●	● ● ● ●	● ● ●
	Overall	● ● ●	● ●	● ● ● ●

4 **Complete the sentences below using the correct form of the adjectives in the box.
The examples in the language box will help you.**

comfortable • expensive •
fast • heavy • noisy •
powerful • safe • spacious •
fast • safe

MAKING COMPARISONS

The VW Passat is **cheaper** than the Audi A4.
This car is **the cheapest** of the three.

A Mercedes is **heavier** than a Smart.
This model is **the heaviest** car in our range.

My new car is **more economical** than the old one.
The Renault is **the most economical** of the cars I looked at.

1   The Audi TT has a top speed of 250 mph. It is much _____ than a Fiat Panda.

2   Rolls-Royce makes some of the _____ cars in the world.

3   All new cars now have airbags as standard so they are _____ than cars were
    years ago.

4   A diesel engine is still _____ than a petrol engine even though they are much
    quieter than they used to be.

5   Volvos have the reputation of being some of the _____ cars on the market.

6   The interior of a Bentley is _____ and luxurious than a BMW 7-series.
    There is even room for a mini bar.

7   The Porsche Cayenne weighs two and a half tonnes. It is _____ than the BMW X5.

8   The Lamborghini Diablo is one of the _____ cars in the world.

9   A car engine with twelve cylinders is _____ than one with six cylinders.

10 These leather seats are the _____ seats I've ever sat in!

5 **Fill in the table below with details about your own car. Then ask two other people in your class
about their cars and complete the table. Use the phrases in the box to help you approximate.**

**After you have completed the table,
compare the three cars.**

APPROXIMATING

It's about/approximately ...	I think it's ...
It's roughly ...	I would guess it's ...
It must be at least ...	I don't know exactly but ...

	Your car	First partner's car	Second partner's car
Acceleration 0–60 mph	_____	_____	_____
Top speed	_____	_____	_____
Fuel consumption	_____	_____	_____
Engine type	_____	_____	_____
Maximum power	_____	_____	_____

AUDIO
25

6 **Listen to the two engineers discussing the dimensions of the car and complete the table.**

Length	
Width	
Height	
Wheel base	
Boot height	

Now work with a partner. First look at the phrases in the box. Then look in the Partner Files and ask each other questions to find the dimensions (1–8) of the car in the drawing below.

TALKING ABOUT DIMENSIONS

How **high/long/wide** is the car/body/... ?
– It's ... millimetres long/high ...
What is the **height/length/width** of the boot/rear overhang/... ?
– The height/width is ... millimetres ...

PARTNER FILES Partner A   File 11, p. 63
Partner B   File 19, p. 65

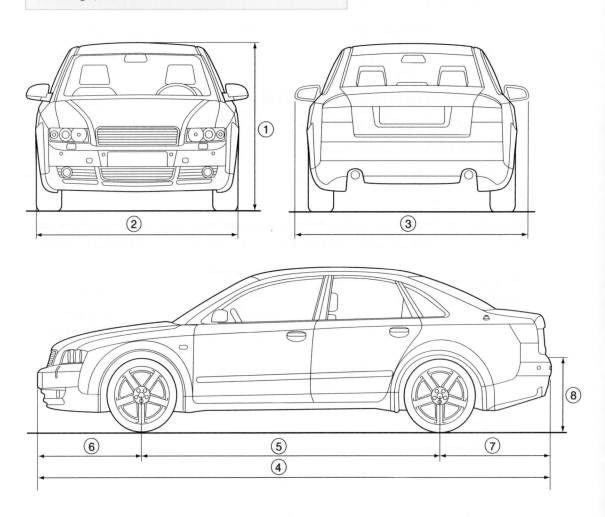

AUDIO
26

7 Which materials are most used in manufacturing a car? Listen to the presentation by a car manufacturer and put them in order.

1st _____

2nd _____

3rd _____

4th = _____

4th = _____

6th _____

7th _____

8th _____

9th _____

> iron • glass • rubber • aluminium
> • steel • other • zinc, lead, and
> copper • fluids and lubricants •
> plastics

Listen again and complete the pie chart.

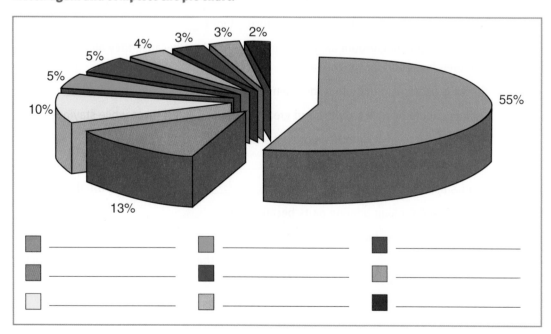

8   **What car parts are made of what material? Work with a partner to complete the table.**

Material	Car part(s)	Material	Car part(s)
aluminium	_____	rubber	_____
foam	_____	sheet metal	_____
glass	_____	steel	_____
leather	_____	textile	_____
magnesium	_____	wood	_____
plastic	_____		

9   **Complete these sentences about materials and their properties using the words in the box.**

> shatterproof • light • corrosion-resistant • durable • elastic • natural • rigid • flammable
> • malleable • heat-resistant

1   Wood is very often used in interiors because it looks _____ and warm.

2   Aluminium and magnesium are important for car makers because they are _____ and therefore good for weight-saving.

3   Safety regulations require that the foam used in car seats shouldn't be _____.

4   Rubber should be able to withstand great temperature differences while staying _____. In other words, it shouldn't become brittle.

5   Windscreens are made of a special _____ glass to protect drivers in accidents.

6   Fabrics used in cars need to be _____ and not look old too quickly.

7   Steel is used for load-bearing parts because it is _____.

8   Sheet metal is used for large car parts because it is _____ and dent-resistant.

9   Ceramic, which is _____, is used in the catalytic converter because of the very high temperatures.

10   Aluminium is ideal for bumpers and other body parts because it is _____.

10 **Work in groups of three to do a meeting role-play.**

You have to decide whether the tailgate of a new car should be made of steel or plastic. Take the parts of a controller (A), a member of the technical department (B), and a member of the production department (C) and try to reach a decision by the end of the meeting.

PARTNER FILES

Partner A File 5, p. 62
Partner B File 16, p. 64
Partner C File 21, p. 65

OUTPUT

Read this article and answer the questions.

Aluminium –
the car maker's metal of the year?

With the launch of the A2, Audi AG introduced the first vehicle in the world to have a volume-built all-aluminium body. In 1996, series production of the A8 began. The A8 is the first luxury limousine made of aluminium, and the Audi plant in Neckarsulm produces 20,000 vehicles a year. The A8 combines high strength with low weight. At only 1,690 kilos, the A8 3.2 is the lightest car in the luxury class. The third-generation Audi Space Frame now has fewer components than its predecessors, which makes it easier to build the car in large quantities.

Other car makers are also starting to take aluminium seriously. As engine sizes have increased, cars have become more top-heavy. Using aluminium for the bonnet and front wings helps to get a better weight distribution between front and rear axles. Another advantage of aluminium is that it is cheaper to recycle than steel. This will be an important consideration in the future when the EU introduces tougher recycling regulations.

But there are drawbacks to using aluminium. Replacing steel with aluminium is expensive; an aluminium body costs twice as much as a steel one. Not only are aluminium production processes expensive, they are also difficult to implement. Because aluminium is more brittle and tears more

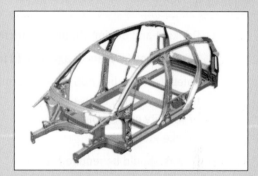

easily than steel, it can only be formed when it is in an unhardened state. Furthermore, the aluminium used for the outer parts of the car, such as the wings and the doors, needs to be thicker than steel because it doesn't have the same stiffness. The dent-resistance of aluminium is also less than that of steel.

On the plus side, aluminium doesn't rust like steel, and in car crashes it has a higher energy absorption rate, which increases the car's active safety.

OVER TO YOU

What are the advantages and disadvantages of using aluminium?

What kind of car materials do you think will be used in the future?

What are the EU's recycling targets for 2015? Do you think car makers will have trouble reaching them?

6 Safety

Do you agree with the following statements? Discuss with a partner.

		Agree	Disagree
1	People should be able to take their driving test when they're 15.	❑	❑
2	Drivers who have just passed their test should have learner plates on their car for the first six months.	❑	❑
3	Drinking and driving should be strictly against the law.	❑	❑
4	Drivers over 65 years of age should take a new test every two years.	❑	❑
5	Safety features like ABS are dangerous – they give drivers a false sense of security and encourage them to take more risks.	❑	❑
6	Drivers should be required to have headlights on during the day.	❑	❑
7	People shouldn't be required to wear seat belts in cars with airbags.	❑	❑
8	Car manufacturers could make cars much safer, if they wanted to.	❑	❑

AUDIO

27

1 Read these extracts from a presentation about a car safety programme and put them in the correct order. Then listen to the presentation to check your answers.

1 ❑ 2 ❑ 3 ❑ 4 ❑

A

This next slide shows the four dummies which are used inside the car in the test. The driver and front passenger dummies not only measure the usual injury criteria, such as head, thorax, pelvic acceleration, and thigh pressure, but also neck pressure, thorax deformation, knee displacement, and lower leg pressure. At the rear are two smaller dummies in children's seats. A further test assesses the injury risk for pedestrians. OK, I think that covers everything about the tests. Now I'd just like to sum up by repeating my main points …

B

... and that brings me on to my next point – the passive vehicle safety programme. This programme has set new standards for passive vehicle safety in Europe and America. Its aim is to provide the customer with an opportunity to compare passive vehicle safety in different car models. Just so that everyone's clear about the terminology, when I say passive vehicle safety, I mean those features used if an accident happens. Features which are used to avoid an accident are referred to as

active vehicle safety. One important feature of the programme is ...

C

... Now we come to the tests themselves. As you can see in this slide, the programme first tested vehicles in a head-on collision with a rigid wall at 64 km/h. In this side-on crash, a 1.5 m wide deformable barrier weighing 950 kg is rammed into the side of the car at 50 km/h. A vehicle can be awarded up to five stars, depending on how it performs in the tests.

D

Good morning everyone. For those of you who don't know me, my name is Gordon Waters. I'm here today to talk about NCAP – that's the New Car Assessment Programme. First of all, I'm going to tell you something about the history of the NCAP. Then I'll talk about the NCAP's passive vehicle safety programme. There'll be time for questions at the end. So, firstly, let's look at the NCAP's history. The NCAP was founded in 1997 and ...

AUDIO

28–33

Now listen to some questions asked by people in the audience. How would you answer them?

2   **Put the safety features into the correct column.**

active safety	passive safety

ABS

adaptive cruise control

crumple zone

highly rigid roof

automatic emergency braking

seat belt

airbags

ESP (Electronic Stability Program)

retractable steering wheel

shatterproof windscreen

lane departure warning system

xenon headlights

Which of these safety features does your car have? Tell your partner.

3   **Work in a small group to discuss safety features.**

You work in the marketing department of a major car manufacturer. Your mid-range model is now entering the fourth year of its eight-year life cycle. Sales have been falling so it is time for an improvement. This car is often bought as a fleet car for business people. You have already agreed on a 'business package' and now want to include one more safety feature. Read the descriptions of the three safety features on the next page, then 'meet' your colleagues to decide which one to include. Try to use the language in the box below.

TALKING ABOUT ADVANTAGES AND DISADVANTAGES	
One great advantage is …	A major drawback/disadvantage is …
I think the … feature is a big plus point.	I can see problems with the …
One point in favour of the … is …	The downside is …

Feature	Advantages	Disadvantages
Traffic Signal Assistant is an audible signal which tells the driver about traffic regulations such as speed limits, parking, or overtaking.	• This would be good marketing for the company as it shows we want considerate drivers who obey rules. • A lot of accidents happen because people drive too fast or overtake on dangerous roads. • Drivers would save money on speeding fines and parking tickets.	• There are already too many traffic signs and regulations regarding speed limits, parking and overtaking. • Business people do not like to be told what to do. • Why are we building such fast cars if this device tells you to slow down all the time?
The 'virtual passenger' voice application wakes up drivers who are beginning to fall asleep. Infrared sensors measure head positions. If the driver's head begins to fall forward, he or she is woken up with a loud greeting and a series of questions to keep him or her awake.	• Business people on long journeys would appreciate this device as many accidents happen because people fall asleep at the wheel. • This technology is not offered by any other car maker as standard and is a good 'gimmick'. • The advertising possibilities would also be good.	• It is too 'gimmicky' for business people. • It is potentially dangerous. Drivers get a false sense of security and may decide to drive even though they are tired or have had alcohol. • If the technology fails and an accident happens, it could cost the company a lot of money. • It is embarrassing for the driver if there are other passengers in the car.
The GPS navigation system helps drivers plan routes and warns drivers about traffic jams and congested roads.	• It is very practical for business people who often go on business trips to different cities. • Accidents are caused by people not knowing where they are going and trying to find the right street. • Avoiding traffic jams and congested roads would save people time and money.	• GPS navigation is no longer anything special. • It needs to be constantly updated, so will be more expensive than other options. • It is only available in great detail for some countries so if the driver is in a country that doesn't have it, it won't help.

4   Choose a safety feature. Work with a partner and prepare a five-minute presentation explaining how your feature works. If you have Internet access, you can visit websites like www.howstuffworks.com to help you. Give your presentation to the class.

MAKING A PRESENTATION

Introducing yourself and your talk
For those of you who don't know me, my name is …
I'm here today to talk about/tell you something about …
I'm going to be speaking about …
Feel free to ask questions as we go along.
There'll be time for questions at the end.

Structuring the presentation
Firstly/Secondly/Thirdly/Finally …
Let's now look at …
Moving on, I'd like to say something about …
Now we come to …

That brings me to my next point.
I think that covers everything about …

Referring to visuals
As you can see in this slide, …
This (next) slide/transparency shows …

Concluding
To sum up …
In conclusion …
I'd just like to repeat my main points.
Are there any questions?

5   **Complete the text about car recalls with a word from the box below.**

charge • dealer • fail • fault • fitted • handbrake • injuries • recall

A leading car manufacturer is recalling 70,000 models in the UK to check for a potentially life-threatening _____[1]. The brake pedal on the top-selling small MPV can _____[2] suddenly.

The problem affects all UK cars sold since the launch in July 2000 except those delivered in recent weeks. A small clip – if incorrectly _____[3] – can allow the pedal to detach from the rest of the braking system. If this happens on the move, the driver is reduced to using the _____[4] and gears to bring the car to a halt.

The car manufacturer says a small number of owners have experienced the problem but no _____[5] have been reported.

The car manufacturer says it has written to every owner asking them to take the car to their _____[6].

Any work needed will be carried out free of _____[7].

Since only 85% of owners respond to _____[8] notices, 10,000 potentially dangerous models could still be left on UK roads.

6   **Work in a small group to have a meeting.**

You are members of the executive board of a major car manufacturer. You have been called to an emergency meeting to discuss a serious problem. One of your best-selling models, the B6, a sports car, has been involved in several accidents. It is unstable at high speeds and drivers cannot control the car. So far no one has been killed, but this could change. First look at the agenda. Then look at your role cards and have the meeting.

Agenda

Emergency meeting to discuss safety problems with the B6.

1 Action
 – Should the model be recalled and fitted with ESP?
 – If so, when?
 – Should customers pay for the work?
 – How should we publicize the recall?

2 Public relations
 – What will the effect of a recall be?
 – What steps can we take to reduce negative publicity?

MEETING PHRASES

Interrupting
Excuse me.
Could I come in here for a moment?
Sorry, can I say something?
I'd like to add something here.

Dealing with interruptions
Hang on a moment.
Can I just finish what I was saying?
We'll come to that point in a moment.
Let me just say one more thing.

PARTNER FILE   Partner A File 6, p. 62   Partner C File 9, p. 63
Partner B File 17, p. 64   Partner D File 22, p. 65

7   Now report on the results of the meeting. Write an email to your subsidiary in France explaining your decision.

OUTPUT   Read the article and answer the questions which follow.

OUR 'AUTO SAFETY' SERIES

THIS MONTH:

Airbags

Until a short time ago, most of the progress made in auto safety was in front and rear accidents, even though 40% of all serious injuries from accidents are the result of side impacts, and 30% of all accidents are side-impact collisions.

Many car makers have reacted to these statistics and new standards of the NHTSA (National Highway Traffic Safety Administration) by making doors, door frames and floor and roof sections stronger. But cars that now offer side airbags represent a new type of occupant protection.

Engineers say that designing effective side airbags is much more difficult than designing front airbags. This is because much of the energy from a front-impact collision is absorbed by the bumper, hood and engine, and it takes almost 30 to 40 milliseconds before the impact reaches the car's occupant. In a side impact, only a relatively thin door and a few inches

separate the occupant from another vehicle. This means that door-mounted side airbags must begin deploying within 5 or 6 milliseconds. It takes a collision of about 19 kph to trigger side air bags.

The seat-belt airbag is intended to give back-seat passengers the same level of protection as front-seat occupants. The airbag is incorporated in the rear-seat seat belt and inflates forward on impact.

Airbags, though, do not always save lives; they sometimes kill people who are too small or are in the wrong position when the airbags deploy. To prevent this from happening, car makers and suppliers are developing occupant-sensing systems. The three leading technologies for smart airbags are weight-sensing in the seat, position sensing within the car, and camera monitoring. These detection systems can automatically deactivate the airbags if the situation is dangerous.

OVER TO YOU

Do you know anyone who has been saved by an airbag in an accident?
Which other safety features are car manufacturers working on at the moment? Which do you think will be developed in the future?
How safe do you feel when driving your car?

7 Design

Say whether you agree or disagree with the statements below (or are not sure). Then discuss your answers with a partner.

Design factors	Agree	Disagree	Not sure
Design is the most important feature of a car.	❑	❑	❑
The colour of the car doesn't matter.	❑	❑	❑
Most cars look pretty much the same.	❑	❑	❑
The drag coefficient has no effect on the design of a car.	❑	❑	❑
As long as the interior looks good, the ergonomics don't matter.	❑	❑	❑
Every car from the same brand should look like part of a family.	❑	❑	❑

1 Look at the descriptions. Which car does each text refer to?

1 The new version of this design classic is as charming as the original. Details such as the steep windscreen and the large round headlights emphasize that this car is unconventional. There's no question that this is a fun car to drive.

2 Its design is a blend of retro and contemporary. It has a sleek, distinctive appearance, with unique proportions and a surprisingly spacious interior. The side profile is muscular and aggressive, and gives the whole vehicle a feeling of motion and direction.

3 This very stylish car has a striking exterior with a compact shape and bold styling. It's a very sporty car with exciting lines and powerful proportions. It features eye-catching details such as the fuel filler cap with its exposed screws.

A PT Cruiser

B Beetle

C Boxster

D Mini

E Audi TT

2   **Look at the adjectives used to describe cars. Put them in the table according to their stress patterns.**

charming • unconventional • muscular • sleek • distinctive • unique •
stylish • striking • contemporary • bold • sporty • spacious

1 syllable	● •	• ●	● • •	• ● •	• • ● • •	• ● • • •

How would you describe the other two cars in exercise 1? Use words from above to write short descriptions.

3   **Cars, and especially car design, are favourite small talk topics. Work in a small group to do the following role-play.**

You (and a colleague) are having dinner in a restaurant together with important customers. Make small talk about your favourite cars. The phrases in the box will help you.

MAKING SMALL TALK

Introducing a topic
One car I really like is the …
I think one of the nicest/most attractive cars on the market is …
I saw a TV programme/read an article about … recently.
Someone told me the other day that …

Keeping the conversation going
What do you think of the … ?
Have you seen the … ?
It's really great/nice/ beautiful/ugly, isn't it?
They must be fun to drive, don't you think?

Changing topic
By the way, …
Anyway, …
That reminds me of …
Speaking of …

AUDIO
34

4 **Listen to the presentation by a car designer and put the six extracts in the correct order.**

1 [c] 2 [ ] 3 [ ] 4 [ ] 5 [ ] 6 [ ]

A

_____ ¹ we also produce a clay model, which has a ratio of 1:4. If it is approved, a 1:1 model is made and presented to a concept clinic. If there are no knock-out factors, the concept goes to a product clinic so that marketing factors can be finalized.

B

_____ ², product planning, marketing, and design come together. Product planning asks 'What could it be?', marketing asks 'Who is it for?', and design asks 'What does it look like?' I should maybe mention at this point that many cars are not really new, but are successors to, or derivatives of, existing models. The design of earlier models naturally needs to be taken into account.

C

_____ ³ taking you through the stages of the design process. There are five phases, which take about three years in total.

D

_____ ⁴ comes series development. The final design is specified. Several prototypes are handmade and tested in various climatic conditions and on different road surfaces.

E

_____ ⁵ is the pre-series phase where the production process and components from suppliers are tried out. A final marketing clinic is carried out to confirm price and market positioning. Then, if everything runs smoothly, there is a design and change freeze. The final phase is series production.

F

_____ ⁶, we have the concept phase where even more people are involved. We need to know what technology will be developed or adapted, which production plant and production processes are necessary, and, finally, financial details such as volume and production costs.

Now listen again and fill the gaps with expressions for ordering a presentation.

Are the following sentences about the presentation true or false?

1 The process of designing a car generally takes three years.
2 Styling only comes into the process when other important decisions have been made.
3 It is necessary to know quite early on in the process which production plant will be used.
4 The number of cars which will be built has no effect on the cost of the final product.
5 The car goes to a product clinic before it goes to a concept clinic.
6 The first model is made of wood.

5 **Match the design vocabulary on the left with the correct definition on the right.**

1	successor	a	the last model
2	derivative	b	limited number of handmade cars with the necessary equipment and technology inside
3	concept car	c	the next model
4	predecessor	d	a limited number of cars built on an assembly line to test tooling and parts
5	design freeze	e	a variation of the basic model
6	prototype	f	the stage where no more design changes are possible
7	pre-series car	g	a car built to show people what the future car will look like (it may have no technology inside)

6 **Describe the process for designing cars in your own words. Look back at Unit 2 for help with describing processes.**

7 **Complete the table. (Hint: the words you need are in exercises 4 and 5.)**

Verb	Noun
to _____ a	adaptation
to _____ b	approval
to assemble	_____ c
to conceive	_____ d
to _____ e	design
to develop	_____ f
to produce	_____ g
to _____ h	specification

Now complete the sentences with words from the table.

1 It won't be necessary to develop new technology for this model. We can _____ what we already have.

2 We need _____ from the Board of Directors if we want to continue with this project.

3 Only models are produced in the _____ clinic, not 'real' cars.

4 The location of the _____ plant has an impact on the pricing of the car.

5 It is necessary to _____ the final design before the prototype is made.

6 Marketing factors, eg target groups and market share, are finalized after a _____ clinic.

8 Some designers are discussing the constraints they work under. Read their comments and match them to the constraints.

> technical requirements • ergonomics • laws • fuel consumption • customer demands • brand identity • recycling • production requirements

1 I can't design any grill I want – it has to look the same on all our cars so people will recognize the brand.

5 I can't use any material I want, no matter how attractive. I have to know if we can use it again.

2 I have to make sure that attractive seats are also comfortable and customers have enough legroom.

6 The car has to be as streamlined as possible so that it doesn't need so much fuel.

3 I have to take safety regulations into account, so I can't put a big metal part on the bonnet which may injure pedestrians.

7 If the customers want cup holders inside the car, I have to put them in.

4 I have to take the size of the engine and other technical parts into account.

8 Sometimes I think of a really great shape for the bonnet and the production guys tell me the metal can't be formed like that.

What constraints do you work under in your job?

9 Work in a small group to have the following meeting.

You work for a major car manufacturer. You are meeting two colleagues to discuss closing the gap in the range of cars you offer. At the moment your product range consists of a compact, a limousine, a large limousine, and a convertible.

The three possibilities for the new model are:
- a small 'green' car (a compact car with no extras and extremely low fuel consumption)
- a roadster (a fun, 'good weather' car for everybody, young and old)
- an SUV (a versatile on-road/off-road vehicle with lots of room)

Think about the advantages and disadvantages of each model and look at your file for some more ideas. Then hold a meeting to discuss which model should be added to the product range. (Look back at Unit 6 for phrases used to talk about advantages and disadvantages.)

PARTNER FILES
Partner A   File 4, p. 62
Partner B   File 18, p. 65
Partner C   File 10, p. 63

Think of the car makers you know and identify a gap in their product range. How would you fill it?

OUTPUT **Read the article and answer the questions which follow.**

Brand DNA

Every car has a brand DNA which makes it distinctive and instantly recognizable. When you see a BMW or Rover, for example, you know exactly what it is. The importance of

national culture in brand DNA is critical, even though global takeovers, mergers, and partnerships are constantly reshaping the car industry. Volvo, based in Sweden, is now owned by an American company, and Britain's Jaguar, Rolls-Royce, and Bentley are no longer British-owned. Chrysler, that most American of manufacturers, is now part of a German company. Spain's Seat and the Czech car maker Skoda are owned by Germany's Volkswagen. And General Motors has controlled Sweden's Saab for a number of years.

Brand DNA consists of corporate identity and an unmistakable design which is influenced by culture. 'Britishness' or 'Frenchness' is important. But how can 'Americanness' or 'Italianness' be defined by a few hundred pounds of sheet metal bent over a frame and set down on four wheels?

To Fiat, Italian means 'sporty'. "People buy Italian cars because they look Italian," said Richard Gadeselli, head of corporate affairs for Fiat Auto S.p.A. "Even the humble Seicento (Fiat's smallest car) has a sporty feel. In everything we design, we try and strive for that. If we took the badges off, people would say, 'I don't know what that is, but it feels Italian'."

Similarly, Japanese design is unmistakably Japanese because of its Zen-like purity and simplicity. Akira Fujimoto, chief editor of Japan's *Car Styling* magazine, says that the level of detail is the key to Japanese design. "With an American car, you can see the differences at 300 metres. With a Japanese car, you see the differences at three metres. Japan is a small country so there's no need to see the differences from far away."

Peter Horbury, chief designer for Volvo Cars, although British himself, says he believes the Swedish essence of Volvo is something the company should keep even if it is owned by Ford Motor Co. But what is Swedishness? "Sweden is known as a caring society," he said. "Swedish cars are safe, practical, and functional and have a timeless quality."

OVER TO YOU

Do you agree that cars from different countries have different styles? If so, what is your favourite national style?

Which country does your car come from? Does it reflect the style of that country?

How would you describe German, Japanese, French, or Italian style?

8 Future trends

How future-oriented are you? Do this quiz and find out.

1 The car will be able to make more intelligent driving decisions than a human can.

- a This is true and the result will be fewer accidents.
- b Surely there are times when people are more intelligent than machines.
- c Driving will be no fun if I can't think for myself.

2 There will be no more switches, only voice control.

- a Great! You don't need to look at the dashboard anymore.
- b Some voice control is OK, but I still want some switches.
- c I prefer switches.

3 The car will be made of self-cleaning materials.

- a No more wasting time at the car wash! This is also good for recycling.
- b Aren't we going to become very lazy?
- c But I want to clean my car! I really enjoy it.

4 Joysticks will replace steering wheels.

- a This is something new and sounds like fun.
- b This could be OK, but it will take me a long time to get used to it.
- c You only need one hand for a joystick. I like having both hands on the steering wheel.

5 Sensors in the car will prevent accidents.

- a This means I can really depend on my car.
- b I would like to turn the sensors on and off when I want.
- c What happens if the sensors don't work?

6 Most of the tasks you do in your office you'll be able to do in your car.

- a This means I won't waste any time on business trips.
- b I'm not sure if I want to think about work all the time.
- c My car is for fun and relaxing, not for work!

Mostly 'a's: Congratulations! You are ready for the future. You are not afraid of change, and you see new technology as a challenge and something positive.

Mostly 'b's: You're not quite ready for the future. You are still asking yourself why changes are necessary instead of accepting that changes are going to happen.

Mostly 'c's: You are fighting against change and new technology. You seem to be afraid of what the future will bring.

1   Read the text about the car of the future. Which of the technical features described are already present in cars today and which still have to be developed? Make a list.

The car of the future

It is a cold winter morning but your car is waiting for you, warm and comfortable, at exactly the temperature you like. You open the door by pressing your finger against the lock and your car greets you with a friendly 'Hi, how are you?' You sit down and the computer reminds you of your schedule. You start the car. You now have a joystick, steering-by-wire, braking-by-wire. The old mechanical parts of the past are gone.

As you back out of your driveway, warning sensors warn you about objects and pedestrians in your way. Using voice commands you programme your route, check your emails and dictate answers, ask for local and international news, look up phone numbers, and play music.

The car also looks after your health. Sensors in your seat and armrest tell you your weight and blood pressure, while sensors in the dashboard notice if you are drowsy and vibrate the joystick to wake you.

Many of the old worries associated with driving are gone. Traffic jams don't happen any more because your car automatically avoids crowded roads. Collision avoidance

Morning James. We're going to Heathrow to catch your flight

sensors prevent accidents. Speeding tickets are also a thing of the past – sensors pick up signals from traffic signs and automatically adjust your speed or stop your car. And breaking down is no longer a problem. Your car diagnoses any potential faults or worn parts and warns you and the service station. When you arrive at the service station, the spare parts are already waiting for you.

Your car can even park itself. Just stop at any parking space (your car knows, of course, if parking is permitted here) and operate the automatic parking system. The car scans the size and shape of the available space and then reverses in.

Are the following sentences about the text true or false?

1   You'll still need a key to open the car door.
2   You'll no longer have a steering wheel.
3   Sensors in the dashboard will measure your blood pressure.
4   You won't be able to fall asleep while driving.
5   You won't need to read traffic signs anymore.
6   You'll still need good parking skills.

2 **Find words and expressions in the text which mean the following:**

1 Spoken instructions to the car
2 Possible problems
3 A recognition system which stops your car from hitting another car
4 Slightly sleepy
5 Congested roads
6 A list of your appointments for the day
7 Fines for driving too fast
8 People on foot

3 **Your boss sends you the following email about the text on page 55. Write a reply.**

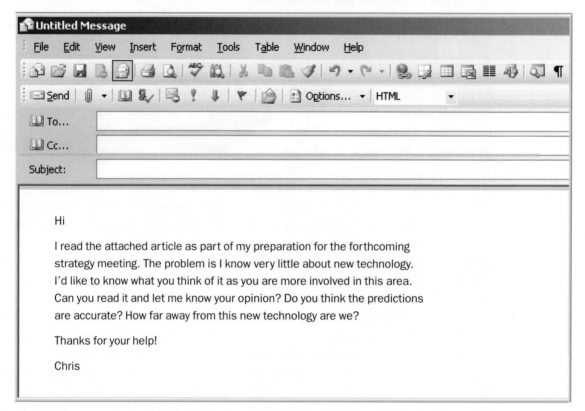

Hi

I read the attached article as part of my preparation for the forthcoming strategy meeting. The problem is I know very little about new technology. I'd like to know what you think of it as you are more involved in this area. Can you read it and let me know your opinion? Do you think the predictions are accurate? How far away from this new technology are we?

Thanks for your help!

Chris

4 **Environmental awareness will become increasingly important in the future. How environmentally-conscious are you?**

Which people in the class do you think would answer 'yes' to the following statements? Ask them and see if you were right.

1 A car's fuel consumption is a key priority when I buy a car.
2 I consider the car's recyclability when I decide which new car to buy.
3 I would be prepared to take part in park & ride or car-sharing schemes.
4 I always find out if my car has been manufactured in a plant with an eco-audit.
5 Fuel should be highly taxed.
6 Introducing a speed limit on roads is a good idea.

5   **You work in the economic and environmental issues department of a major car maker. You have heard that the government plans to introduce a speed limit on motorways in the future to come in line with the rest of Europe. You are meeting to discuss whether or not to support this measure.**

Group A You are *for* introducing a speed limit. Brainstorm arguments in favour of the speed limit, then check the Partner File for more ideas.

Group B You are *against* introducing a speed limit. Brainstorm arguments against the speed limit, then check the Partner File for more ideas.

> **PARTNER FILES**   Group A   File 8, p. 63
> Group B   File 20, p. 65

AUDIO
35–38

6   **Listen to four people speaking about the future of cars. Match the speaker and the topic of their presentation.**

1   Eleonora Gentile ☐

2   Uwe Schmidt ☐

3   Pascal Callabat ☐

4   Cathy Epson ☐

a   the intelligent car of the future
c   new market possibilities in China

b   telematics
d   swivelling headlights

Now listen again and complete the sentences.

1   The level of car _____ is expected to rise to 50 million by the end of this decade.
2   The solid line represents sales with the headlights as _____ .
3   You may feel afraid of the new technology and the fact that the car will make decisions that _____ now make.
4   We are offering voice-activated _____ , constant traffic monitoring and, of course, SOS assistance.

Which speaker is ...

1   at the beginning of the presentation?
2   somewhere in the middle?

3   referring to a graph?
4   at the end of the presentation?

Note phrases from the presentations that support your answer.

7 **Match words from the two boxes to find expressions from exercise 6.**

> absolutely • best • car • dotted •
> highly • joint • main • significant

> venture • development • competitor • option
> • line • probable • ownership • certain

Now use the expressions above to complete the sentences.

1 We have a number of choices but our _____ is to lower fuel consumption.

2 On the next slide, the _____ indicates the money saved by using recycled materials.

3 At the beginning of the year we formed a _____ with a company in Africa.
   We're _____ that this was the right decision.

4 The most _____ last year was in the lowering of emissions.

5 _____ is clearly rising in the Far East as more and more people can afford
   vehicles and fuel.

6 I'm not 100% sure but it is _____ that our _____ is coming
   out with an environmentally friendly model within the next five years.

8 **The phrases below are used to talk about the future. First put them in the table.**

> without doubt • is expected to • I'm absolutely certain • there's a good
> chance • it is quite likely • you may feel • there's no doubt that • we are
> convinced • it's highly probable

certainty	probability	possibility
without doubt	_____	_____
_____	_____	_____
_____	_____	
_____		

**Now use the phrases to discuss the following statements in small groups. Do you think these
things will happen in the next five/ten/twenty years?**

India will be a major market.
Cars will use only one litre of petrol per 100 km.
Sports cars will have a top speed of more than 300 km/h.
Cars will be like offices with on-board computers and email facilities.
Cars will have an auto pilot.
Cars will be almost 100% recyclable.
Environmentally friendly cars will be more important.

9   **Work with a partner. Prepare a short presentation on one of these topics. (Look back at Unit 6 for help with presentation language.)**

- The future of my company/our product lines
- Future developments in the global car market
- Fuels of the future
- The car of the future

Give your presentation to your class. Do they agree with your predictions?

OUTPUT   **Read the text and answer the questions which follow.**

Fuel cells

The use of fuel cells promises a reduction in environmental pollution from car exhaust emissions, and the end of our dependence on oil for fuel.

A fuel cell produces an electric current and heat by converting hydrogen and oxygen into water. The output of a single cell is 0.6–0.8 V, but when many cells are combined into a stack, enough energy is produced to power a 50 kW engine.

The fuel cell has the highest efficiency in power generation, reaching over 60%, compared to a gasoline-powered car which has 20%.

The oxygen required comes from the air, but hydrogen is not so readily available. Pure hydrogen could be stored on-board the car, but this would use too much space. Alternatively, car makers could use reformer technology to convert gasoline or methanol into hydrogen, but this would reduce the efficiency of the cell.

For drivers there are many practical considerations. Fuel cell-powered cars are neither as fast nor as quiet as gasoline- or diesel-powered cars. At present there are very few hydrogen fuelling stations, so refuelling could be a problem. Fuel cell cars have a shorter range, so drivers will have to refuel more often. If a tank of hydrogen is stored on board, there are problems of space and safety.

Fuel cell cars are very expensive to

develop and produce, which means they will also be expensive for the customer. Many drivers will not pay extra for 'green' car technology, especially if it is not as convenient as the current system. Nevertheless, the race is on to produce the first fuel cell-powered family car with CO_2 emissions of 90 g/km (equivalent to gasoline consumption of 3.0 l/100 km).

OVER TO YOU

How does fuel cell technology work?

What are the advantages and disadvantages of fuel cell-powered cars?

How important do you think fuel cell cars are or will become?

Would you buy a fuel cell car? Why or why not?

Test yourself!

See how much 'automobile' vocabulary you've learned.
Use the clues to complete the crossword puzzle.

Across

1   How much a car weighs when there are no passengers in it and with half a tank of fuel. (British English – 2 words – 4, 6)

6   You put your foot on this pedal when you change gears.

10   The marketing department wants these people to buy the car. (2 words – 6, 5)

11   SCEVOSRRO: A car which combines the features of an SUV, a MPV, and a saloon.

14   The next model.

20   How much petrol or diesel the car uses: *fuel* ... .

21   Another word for passenger.

22   A mixture of metals.

24   To drive backwards.

26   The instruments and other buttons are located here.

28   Gases, etc. that are sent out into the air (especially through the exhaust pipe).

30   This is found on the instrument panel and shows how hot the engine is: ... *gauge*.

31   A type of fuel; the BE word for *gas(oline)*.

Down

2   How much your car is worth when you want to sell it. (2 words – 6, 5)

3   You fill this with petrol.

4   You operate this when you park the car.

5   This pedal makes the car go faster.

7   This means the car has a lot of room for passengers.

8   This regulates your speed so you don't have to put your foot on the accelerator. (2 words – 6, 7)

9   BCLIATNUR: This protects moving parts in the engine and stops friction.

12   A long line of vehicles on a road that cannot move or only very slowly. (2 words – 7, 3)

13   Cars are built on this. (2 words – 8, 4)

15   The fastest your car can go. (2 words – 3, 5)

16   This means the material lasts for a long time.

17   A car which doesn't use much fuel is this.

18   A car with a lot of space behind the back seats; the BE word for station wagon: ... *car*.

19   The rotational force generated by the engine.

23   The car's capacity to go fast or accelerate quickly.

25   This is inflated to protect you in an accident.

26   You measure the engine oil with this.

27   You open this to look at the engine.

29   This ignites the air/fuel mixture in the combustion chamber. (2 words – 5, 4)

Partner Files

Unit 2, Exercise 13   File 1 ⬅

Partner A

Phone call 1: You are Alex. Call the bulb supplier (a Spanish company called AutoLux) to complain about the problem with the bulbs. Ask what they are going to do to prevent the problem happening again.

Phone call 2: You are Alex. Call Chris to explain what the problem with the headlights was, and say what you are going to do to solve the problem.

Unit 3, Exercise 5   File 2 ⬅

Partner A

You don't want to remove the cigarette lighter and ashtray.

- The lighter and ashtray are standard equipment for every car maker.
- A lot of people in your country smoke – and don't forget the marketing slogan: 'Don't teach the customer!'
- It will be expensive for the supplier to produce one part with an ashtray, for example, and one part without. So costs will go up.

Unit 4, Exercise 9   File 3 ⬅

Partner A

You are visiting a trade fair in England. You are interested in a major car company's new 808 model. Ask questions about:

- price
- the engine
- fuel consumption
- optional extras

Unit 7, Exercise 9   File 4 ⬅

Partner A

▲ = Advantage
▼ = Disadvantage

Small 'green' car

▲ Less fuel consumption means less pollution.
▲ Not every car maker has this sort of car. It will show our expertise.
▼ There can be no extras such as air conditioning because of weight-saving.

Roadster

▲ It will appeal to men and women and attract young people to the brand.
▼ It is a 'good weather' car which people will only want in summer.

SUV

▲ It gives drivers a feeling of safety because it is a big, 'muscular' car.
▼ It is too big for most garages and parking spaces.
▼ SUVs are bad for the environment.

Unit 5, Exercise 10   File 5 ⬅

Partner A – Controller

- Your task is to find out which material is the most cost-effective for the company.
- You need to produce 100 pieces per day.
- Good design is a USP (unique selling point) of your company.

Unit 6, Exercise 6   File 6 ⬅

Partner A – Assistant to the CEO

You are the chairperson.
- It is your job to start the meeting and say what it is about.
- Remember to summarize any points agreed on and to keep order.
- You are also responsible for concluding the meeting.

Unit 4, Exercise 5   File 7 ⬅

Partner A

1 engine oil dipstick
2 battery
3 brake fluid reservoir
4 engine oil filler cap
5 radiator expansion tank
6 power steering reservoir
7 windscreen/headlight washer container

Unit 8, Exercise 5   File 8 ⬅

Group A

- There would be fewer accidents and less aggressive driving if there were a speed limit.
- There would be lower fuel consumption and less pollution.
- Cars are actually cheaper to produce if they're not equipped for high speeds. Those savings could be passed on to the customer.

Unit 6, Exercise 6   File 9 ⬅

Partner C – Director of Marketing

- You feel it doesn't matter if it's the car's or the driver's fault.
- Accidents have happened and the company has to react before there is too much negative publicity.
- It's best to recall the cars as quickly as possible and fit them with ESP at the company's expense.
- You cannot tell customers that they can't drive properly even if it is the truth.

Unit 7, Exercise 9   File 10 ⬅

Partner C

▲ = Advantage
▼ = Disadvantage

Small 'green' car

▲ Advertising this environmentally friendly car would make the company look good.
▼ A low-weight car is expensive to produce and expensive to buy. Customers will not pay the higher price.

Roadster

▲ People want sporty cars with powerful engines.
▼ It is very expensive for young people.

SUV

▲ It is a good car for the American market (export).
▼ Most car makers have a roadster in the product range so it is nothing special.
▼ An SUV is bulky and heavy, and has very high fuel consumption.

Unit 5, Exercise 6   File 11 ⬅

Partner A

Height – 1428 mm
Body width – 1766 mm
Rear overhang – 976 mm
Boot height – 694 mm

Ask about: body width including mirrors, length, wheel base, and front overhang.

Unit 2, Exercise 13   File 12

Partner B

Phone call 1: You work for AutoLux. Deal with Alex's complaint as politely and professionally as you can.

Phone call 2: You are Chris. Make a note of what Alex tells you. Make sure (s)he gives you exact information about what (s)he is going to do to solve the problem, and when (s)he will solve it.

Unit 3, Exercise 5   File 13

Partner B

You want to remove the cigarette lighter and ashtray.
- Many customers don't smoke and don't want people to smoke in their cars.
- The resale value of a non-smoker car is higher than for a smoker.
- The space can be used for other features, for example a money box (instead of the ashtray) and a pen or drink holder (instead of the cigarette lighter).

Unit 4, Exercise 5   File 14

Partner B

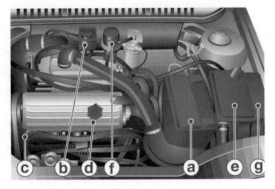

a battery
b brake fluid reservoir
c engine oil dipstick
d engine oil filler cap
e radiator expansion tank
f power steering reservoir
g windscreen/headlight washer container

Unit 4, Exercise 9   File 15

Partner B

You work in the sales department of a British car company and are working at your company's stand at a trade fair. Answer the visitor's questions as best you can. Here is some information about the new 808 model.

- 6-cylinder in-line engine
- 15.7 mpg urban fuel consumption
- optional extras: parking heating, active seats, 3D navigation, sport suspension
- £36,120 for the saloon, £38,430 for the estate

Unit 5, Exercise 10   File 16

Partner B – Technical Department

- The steel tailgate can be painted with the body, but the plastic cannot. This involves more work and problems with matching colours afterwards.
- The plastic tailgate needs to be recycled separately.
- Plastic parts cannot be produced in great quantities because the production cycle time is longer. If you want to produce more than 100 parts per day, you need another set of tools.
- Steel is cheaper than plastic.

Unit 6, Exercise 6   File 17

Partner B – Director of Technical Development

- You believe it is entirely the driver's fault.
- In-company tests have found no technical faults with the car.
- This is a relatively cheap sports car, and customers who don't have enough money for a Porsche buy this one. These customers are simply driving too fast.
- The company should hold a press conference to explain the above point.
- The company can offer driver training at a special price but doesn't need to take any further action.

Unit 7, Exercise 9   File 18

Partner B

▲ = Advantage
▼ = Disadvantage

Small 'green' car

▲ The company needs a car for the 'green' target group. These people are not interested in high-performance cars, but want a car that fits their lifestyle.
▼ Not enough people are really interested in the environment.

Roadster

▲ There is a lot of potential for exciting advertising.
▼ This is an expensive car with a very limited target group.
▼ It is noisy when you drive fast.

SUV

▲ It is spacious and good for transporting things.
▼ Drivers seldom need the off-road functions.

Unit 5, Exercise 6   File 19

Partner B

Length – 4547 mm
Body width including mirrors – 1937 mm
Front overhang – 921 mm
Wheel base – 2650 mm

Ask about: boot height, height, body width, and rear overhang.

Unit 8, Exercise 5   File 20

Group B

- Your company is well-known for its sporty cars. A speed limit would limit personal freedom and the right to drive as fast as you want.
- If drivers can't drive really fast, why build powerful engines and aerodynamic cars?
- There are already enough rules and regulations.

Unit 5, Exercise 10   File 21

Partner C – Production Department

- Plastic parts are injection-moulded so we can get exactly the design we want.
- Lower weight is better for fuel consumption.
- The tools for making plastic parts are cheaper.
- Plastic has the same dent-resistant properties as steel.

Unit 6, Exercise 6   File 22

Partner D – Director of Production

- You believe there is no technical problem.
- The company should wait and see what happens.
- In a couple of weeks the newspapers will forget about the story.
- If the company recalls the cars and fits them with ESP, it's a sign that the company has made a mistake and more cases will be reported.

Answer key

Unit 1

page 5

1 status symbol: Gertrude
lifestyle product: Giles
functional product: Michael
danger to the environment: Pauline
1 colour, interior
2 brand, boot
3 engine, equipment
4 transport, exhaust

page 6

2 1 d   2 a   3 f   4 g   5 b   6 e   7 c

page 7

4 a coupe
b estate (car)
c limousine
d convertible
e pick up
f hatchback
g SUV
h sports car
i saloon

Note: An MPV is also called a people carrier in the UK and a minivan in the USA.

Suggested answers
1 estate car, hatchback, limousine, SUV
2 pick up, SUV
3 hatchback, convertible, coupe, pick up, sports car
4 convertible
5 hatchback
6 hatchback
7 sports car, convertible
8 estate car, MPV, pick up

page 8

5

Driver airbag	Yes
Passenger airbag	Yes
Lateral airbags	No
ABS	Yes
No. of cylinders	4
mpg	40
Top speed	140
CD-autochanger	Yes
Satellite navigation	Yes
Sports steering wheel	No
Leather seats	No

6 1 b   2 d   3 a   4 h   5 f   6 c
7 e   8 g

page 9

1 resale value
2 standard equipment
3 diesel engine
4 crash tests
5 brand image
6 fuel consumption
7 passenger airbags
8 leather seats

7 Suggested answers
1 coupe or a roadster
2 estate or MPV
3 limousine or sports car
4 estate or MPV
5 hatchback
6 sports car or convertible

page 10

10 1 resale value
2 engine
3 performance
4 pollution
5 fuel consumption
6 top speed
7 price
8 brand
9 safety
The expensive type of car is LIMOUSINE.

Unit 2

page 12

Starter
1 BMW
2 Vauxhall
3 VW
4 Mercedes
5 Porsche
6 Mini

1 1 sunroof
2 roof
3 windscreen
4 windscreen wiper
5 bonnet
6 logo
7 headlight
8 front bumper
9 indicator
10 wing
11 wheel arch
12 sill
13 tyre
14 wheel trim
15 petrol flap

page 13

16 wing mirror
17 side window
18 aerial
19 rear window
20 badge

21 number plate
22 boot
23 rear bumper
24 exhaust pipe
25 rear light
26 door
27 door handle

2 1 bonnet
2 bumpers
3 aerial
4 boot
5 windscreen wipers/headlights
6 badge/logo
7 tyres
8 logo
9 sunroof
10 indicator

3 1 headlights
2 brake lights
3 exhaust pipe
4 wheel trim
5 front bumper
6 petrol cap
7 windscreen wipers
8 wing mirror
9 door handle
10 number plate

page 14

4 1 E – number plate
2 B – brake lights
3 D – petrol cap
4 A – wing mirror
5 C – exhaust pipe

page 15

5 a delivery date
b (weekly and daily) Production schedules
c (the company's own) pre-assembly stations
d Data carrier
e floor pan
f wheel arches
g roof
h Add-on parts
i paint shop
j final assembly
k Quality control
l Finished car

6 1 is produced
2 are sold
3 can be placed
4 are assembled
5 can be bought
6 are designed
7 should be replaced

page 16

8 The correct order is: e, b, h, i, f, j, d, g, a, c

page 17

11 1 e   2 b   3 a   4 c   5 h   6 d
7 g   8 i   9 f

There is an unacceptable failure rate of around 5 per cent with the consignment of headlights.

Possible causes for the problem could include a problem with the manufacturing process, or faulty components from the manufacturer's suppliers.

12 1 How's it going?
2 I'm calling about ... .
3 ... can you give it to me again ... ?
4 Let me just read that back to you.
5 After that you can reach me ... .
6 I'll call you as soon as I know something.
7 Speak to you later.

page 18

14 1 c   2 d   3 a   4 e   5 f   6 b   7 h   8 g

Unit 3

page 20

1 1 sun visor
2 airbag
3 steering wheel
4 horn
5 dashboard
6 ignition
7 rear-view mirror
8 hands-free telephone
9 cigarette lighter
10 glove compartment
11 air vent
12 door handle
13 door tray
14 car seat (headrest)
15 seat belt
16 cup holder
17 handbrake
18 gearstick
19 ashtray
20 accelerator
21 brake pedal
22 clutch pedal

page 21

2 1 cup holder
2 clutch pedal
3 sun visor
4 steering wheel
5 hands-free telephone
6 glove compartment
7 cigarette lighter
8 air vent

3 1 engine oil temperature gauge
2 rev counter
3 warning/indicator lights
4 coolant temperature gauge
5 fuel gauge
6 speedometer
7 voltmeter
8 driver information system

4 1 speedometer
2 engine oil temperature gauge
3 indicator lights
4 rev counter
5 fuel gauge
6 voltmeter

page 22

6 Suggested answer
1 Adjust seat (if necessary)
2 Check position of steering wheel and adjust if necessary
3 Check positions of rear-view and side mirrors and adjust if necessary
4 Switch on the headlights if dark
5 Fasten seat belt

7 1 seat belt
2 pedals
3 rear-view
4 headlights
5 ignition

page 23

8 *Open/Close*
bonnet
boot
door
petrol cap
glove compartment
sunroof

Adjust
rear-view mirror
headrest
seat height
seat position
seat belt
side mirror
steering wheel
tyre pressure

Switch on/off
fog lights
headlights
indicator
windscreen wipers

Check
oil level
fuel
tyre pressure
rear-view mirror
seat position
side mirror

9 1 Switch on the fog lights.
2 Adjust the seat height.
3 Check the oil level.
4 Open the door.
5 Adjust the rear-view mirror.
6 Switch on the headlights.
7 Open the bonnet.
8 Adjust the steering wheel.
9 Check the tyre pressure.
10 Open the glove compartment.
11 Open the sunroof.
12 Adjust the seat position.

page 24

10 1 writing
2 Unfortunately
3 possible
4 appreciate
5 sending
6 attachment
7 forward

page 25

11 1 c   2 f   3 e   4 d   5 b   6 a

A Safety/Technology
B Seats
C Audio/Communication
D Wheels/Tyres
E Interior equipment
F Exterior equipment

page 26

12 Across
1 ashtray
3 dashboard
5 brake
8 sun visor
9 gearstick

Down
2 headrest
4 handbrake
6 glove
7 mirror

Unit 4

page 27

Starter
1 front-wheel drive
2 brake horsepower
3 grams per kilometre
4 Gasoline Direct Injection
5 miles per gallon
6 miles per hour
7 Newton metre
8 revolutions per minute
9 rear-wheel drive
10 spark ignition
11 turbo direct injection

1 1 piston
2 crankshaft
3 engine
4 clutch
5 gearbox
6 propeller shaft

page 28

2 1 combustion
2 fuel
3 spark plug
4 piston
5 crankshaft
6 torque
7 cylinders
8 clutch
9 distribution

page 29

3 a power
b powerful
c combustion
d ignite
e explode
f explosion
g rotate
h rotational
i transmit

1 rotational
2 transmitted
3 ignites; explosion
4 powerful
5 combustion

4 1 V-engine
2 horizontally opposed engine
3 in-line engine

page 30

6 1 f   2 g   3 b   4 a   5 e   6 c   7 d

page 31

7 The order in which the key features are mentioned is:
1 b design
2 g increased power of the engine
3 d six-speed automatic gearbox as standard
4 c top speed
5 f acceleration from 0–60 in 6 seconds
6 a low fuel consumption
7 e optional extras included in the price

The numbers refer to:
1 engine size in litres
2 engine power in brake horse power
3 top speed in miles per hour
4 the new engines available later in the year
5 fuel consumption around town in miles per gallon
6 fuel consumption for everyday driving
7 price in pounds
8 wheel size in inches

1 Because it is beautiful. / Because of the design.
2 Because it is light. / Because it is made of aluminium.
3 Brochure and card. To encourage the visitor to find out more about the car and maybe to buy it.

page 32

8 1 d   2 f   3 b   4 a   5 c   6 e

10 **Across**
1 fluid
3 fuel
5 coolant
7 crankshaft
10 oil
11 battery

Down
2 diesel
4 piston
5 cylinder
6 washer
8 acid
9 spark plug

Unit 5

page 34

Starter
1 Lamborghini
2 Mini
3 BMW 7-series

1 not mentioned
b top speed   d body strength   j chassis length

1 c   2 h   3 k   4 i   5 g   6 f   7 a   8 e

page 35

1 True
2 False: The running costs are lower.
3 False: The urban consumption is low.
4 True

2 1 urban consumption
2 Cd value
3 running costs
4 resale value
5 braking distance
6 boot capacity
7 front suspension
8 disc brakes
9 kerb weight

1 d   2 a   3 b   4 f   5 h   6 c
7 g   8 e   9 i

page 36

3 a car 1   e car 1
b car 1   f car 3
c car 2   g car 1
d car 2

page 37

4 1 faster
2 most expensive
3 safer
4 noisier
5 safest
6 more spacious
7 heavier
8 fastest
9 more powerful
10 most comfortable

page 38

6

Length	4993mm
Width	1857mm
Height	1398mm
Wheel base	2885mm
Boot height	690mm

page 39

7 1st steel
2nd iron
3rd plastics
4th = aluminium
4th = rubber
6th fluids and lubricants
7th zinc, lead and copper
8th other
9th glass

■ steel (55%)
■ iron (13%)
▢ plastics (10%)
■ aluminium (5%)
■ rubber (5%)
▢ fluids and lubricants (4%)
■ zinc, lead, and copper (3%)
■ other (fabrics, ceramics) (3%)
■ glass (2%)

page 40

8 Suggested answers

aluminium: car body, car parts, wheel trim, engine parts

foam: seats, padded interior parts

glass: windscreen, windows, mirrors

leather: seat covers, steering wheel

magnesium: engine parts, gearbox parts, steering column components

plastic: body parts, interior parts, dashboard, gear stick

rubber: tyres, body stripping, pedal covering

sheet metal: body parts

steel: body parts, wheel trim, axle parts, suspension, engine parts

textile: seat covers, interior covers

wood: dashboard

9
1 natural	6 durable
2 light	7 rigid
3 flammable	8 malleable
4 elastic	9 heat-resistant
5 shatterproof	10 corrosion-resistant

Unit 6

page 42

1 The correct order is: D, B, C, A

page 43

Suggested answers

1 No, sorry. I said it only tests *passive* safety.
2 It provides information for consumers.
3 It's 64 kilometres per hour.
4 No, I said that new cars are given a *star* rating.
5 Yes, that's right.
6 No, there's also a test which assesses the injury risk for *pedestrians*.

page 44

2 active safety
ABS
adaptive cruise control
automatic emergency braking
ESP
lane departure warning system
xenon headlights

passive safety
airbags
crumple zone
highly rigid roof
retractable steering wheel
seat belt
shatterproof windscreen

page 46

5
1 fault	5 injuries
2 fail	6 dealer
3 fitted	7 charge
4 handbrake	8 recall

Unit 7

page 48

1 1 Mini (D)   2 PT Cruiser (A)   3 Audi TT (E)

page 49

2

1 syllable	●•	•●	●••	•●•	••●••	•●•••
sleek	charming	unique	muscular	distinctive	unconventional	contemporary
bold	stylish					
	striking					
	sporty					
	spacious					

Model answers

Beetle: The distinctive shape of this VW sedan gave the car its name. The original car, produced in 1939, had an air-cooled engine and was very inexpensive. The new model is just as charming as the old and has many of the same unconventional features.

Boxster: A sleek, elegant car with a contemporary design but one can feel and see the tradition in this famous sports car. The car has the pure spirit of a roadster and promises a fantastic driving experience.

page 50

4 The correct order is: C, B, F, A, D, E
1 In the concept phase	2 First of all
3 We'll start by	4 After the concept phase
5 After that	6 Secondly

1 True
2 False: Styling is discussed during the first meeting.
3 True
4 False: Volume does affect the cost.
5 False: The concept clinic is first.
6 False: It's made of clay.

page 51

5 1 c   2 e   3 g   4 a   5 f   6 b   7 d

7
a adapt	e design
b approve	f development
c assembly	g product/production
d concept	h specify

1 adapt	4 assembly/production
2 approval	5 specify
3 concept	6 product

page 52

8 1 brand identity   5 recycling
   2 ergonomics   6 fuel consumption
   3 laws   7 customer demands
   4 technical requirements 8 production
                                   requirements

Unit 8

page 55

1 1 False: You'll just need to touch the lock.
   2 True
   3 False: The sensors are in the seat and armrest.
   4 True
   5 True
   6 False: The car will be able to park itself.

page 56

2 1 voice commands
   2 potential faults
   3 collision avoidance sensors
   4 drowsy
   5 traffic jams
   6 schedule
   7 speeding tickets
   8 pedestrians

page 57

6 1 c   2 d   3 a   4 b

   1 ownership   2 standard
   3 drivers   4 navigation

   1 Cathy Epson (Hello. My name's Cathy Epson from
      Elite Satellite.)
   2 Inge Beck (Let's now turn to …) or Uwe Schmidt
      (Let's move on to …)
   3 Uwe Schmidt (The solid line represents …/The
      dotted line indicates …/The blue-coloured line
      shows …)
   4 Pascal Callabat (So, that brings me to the end of
      my talk today.)

page 58

7 1 best option
   2 dotted line
   3 joint venture; absolutely certain
   4 significant development
   5 Car ownership
   6 highly probable; main competitor

8 **certainty**
   without doubt
   I'm absolutely certain
   there's no doubt that
   we are convinced

   probability
   is expected to
   it is quite likely
   it's highly probable

   possibility
   there's a good chance
   you may feel

page 61

Test yourself!

Across		Down	
1	kerb weight	2	resale value
6	clutch	3	tank
10	target group	4	handbrake
11	crossover	5	accelerator
14	successor	7	spacious
20	consumption	8	cruise control
21	occupant	9	lubricant
22	alloy	12	traffic jam
24	reverse	13	assembly line
26	dashboard	15	top speed
28	emissions	16	durable
30	temperature	17	economical
31	petrol	18	estate
		19	torque
		23	performance
		25	airbag
		26	dipstick
		27	bonnet
		29	spark plug

Transcripts

UNIT 1, EXERCISE 1

Giles

For me the car is a part of my personality. It gives a message to other people about who I am and what I believe in. The colour and the interior features are very important. I put a lot of thought into the car I buy – it has to be me.

Michael

How do I see the car? It's just a piece of metal on four wheels. I just want it to get me from A to B, that's all. Of course if it's comfortable and safe, that's great, but I really don't care about the brand. I'm only interested in details such as the price, fuel consumption, how many seats there are, and how big the boot is.

Gertrude

The car gives me prestige. I would only buy an expensive car with a powerful engine and all the latest equipment. I have a lot of money and why shouldn't I show it? I have a beautiful house and I need an expensive car in the garage.

Pauline

Well, I have a car because I live in the country and there's no public transport. But I think cars are polluting the world. Just think of all the exhaust gases! And what do you do with a car at the end of its life? You can't recycle all of it.

UNIT 1, EXERCISE 5

Salesman	I see you're interested in this model.
John	Yes, we're looking for a car for our son. He's just passed his test.
Alison	We want a car with good safety features that's also economical.
Salesman	Well, you're right, this car would be ideal for your son. It's fully equipped with driver and passenger airbags and has a very good result in crash tests. And ABS is standard equipment.
John	And lateral airbags?
Salesman	No, I'm afraid not.
John	What about fuel consumption?
Salesman	It depends on the engine. Do you want a diesel or a petrol engine? The diesel is more expensive, but more economical.
John	I don't think my son will drive long distances so we'll go for the petrol engine.
Salesman	Then I would recommend the 4 cylinder petrol engine. It has a fuel consumption of 40 miles per gallon, that's approximately 6 litres per one hundred kilometres. And its top speed is 140 mph.
Alison	This company has a good name for quality, doesn't it? I like their cars.
Salesman	That's right. You can't go wrong with this one. And a good brand image is important when you want to sell your car. The resale value is still very high after three years.

	Now would you like to sit in the car and have a closer look at the interior?
John	What does the price include?
Salesman	A CD-autochanger comes as standard and we are also giving away a free satellite navigation system.
Alison	I'm not sure about this steering wheel, or the leather seats.
Salesman	That's the sports version. I'm sure your son would like them, but they do cost extra. Now, we can go through all the options together. Have you thought about the colour?

UNIT 2, EXERCISE 4

Speaker 1

This shows the registration of your car.

Speaker 2

These show motorists behind you whether you are slowing down or stopping.

Speaker 3

You need to open this first so you can fill the tank.

Speaker 4

You need to adjust this so you can see the traffic behind you.

Speaker 5

The exhaust gases from the engine come out of this.

UNIT 2, EXERCISE 8

Put the vehicle into gear (manual transmission) or park (automatic).
Take the spare tyre out of the boot and make sure it is in good condition.
Find two rocks or large pieces of wood and put them in front of and behind the opposite wheel.
Loosen the wheel nuts slightly.
Use a jack to raise the vehicle.
Loosen the wheel nuts more and remove them.
Remove the tyre and put it under the vehicle, next to the jack.
Fit the spare tyre and tighten the wheel nuts.
Remove the old tyre from under the vehicle and lower the vehicle.
Check again to make sure the wheel nuts are tight.

UNIT 2, EXERCISE 11

Alex	Halla Systems. Alex Newman speaking.
Chris	Hi, Alex. It's Chris Fraser here from Rover.
Alex	Ah, hi Chris. How's it going?
Chris	Fine, thanks. Listen Alex I'm calling about the headlights we received from you last week.
Alex	Uh huh. Is there a problem with the headlights?
Chris	I'm afraid there is. In our tests there's been a much higher failure rate than is allowed in the contract.
Alex	Oh dear. I'm sorry to hear that. Can you tell me what the failure rate is exactly?

Chris	Its around 5 percent. And as you know, it should be under 1 percent.
Alex	You're right, that's completely unacceptable. Could you just give me the consignment number, please?
Chris	Sure. It's A348.
Alex	Got you. OK Chris, this is what I'm going to do. I'll look into the problem straight away and will get back to you as soon as I can.
Chris	That's really good of you, Alex. Ill be in my office until about 4 p.m. After that you can reach me on my mobile.
Alex	OK. I think I've got your mobile number, but can you give it to me again just in case?
Chris	Yes. Its 0044 795 434 5381.
Alex	Let me just read that back to you. 0044 795 434 5381 – is that right?
Chris	Yes, that's right.
Alex	Great, OK Chris, like I said, I'll call you as soon as I know something. Bye now.
Chris	Thanks, Alex. Speak to you later.

UNIT 3, EXERCISE 7

🌀 14

Instructor	OK, so you're sitting in the car. What do you do now?
Learner	Well, I start the car. No, wait! I check behind me first before I drive away.
Instructor	You've forgotten something.
Learner	Of course, I fasten my seat belt first.
Instructor	Even before you fasten your seat belt there are things you need to do. First of all, are you sitting comfortably?
Learner	Not really. The seat is a bit too far from the pedals.
Instructor	So you need to adjust the seat, right? Use the two levers there to adjust the position and the height. You can also adjust the steering wheel. So now you're sitting comfortably. What should you check now?
Learner	That the rear-view mirror is in the right position. And the side mirror.
Instructor	Quite right. What next?
Learner	Well, if it's dark, I need to switch on the headlights.
Instructor	Good. Finally, before you put the key into the ignition, what should you do?
Learner	Now I fasten my seat belt.

UNIT 4, EXERCISE 2

🌀 15

Now we come to the engine. The principle of the internal combustion engine has not changed in the last 100 years. The engine takes in fuel and air which is compressed in a combustion chamber. Then, this mixture is ignited by a spark plug to produce an explosion, which moves the piston in the cylinder. The up and down motion of the piston in the cylinder is converted into rotational motion by the crankshaft. The rotational force generated by the engine is known as torque. The size of the engine determines the power. The more cylinders there are, the more powerful the engine. This power is transmitted through the clutch, the gearbox, the propeller shaft (in rear-wheel and four-wheel drive), and the axles to the wheels. The position of the engine can vary, but generally speaking it is mounted at the front. In some sports cars, the engine is mounted at the rear, for example Porsche, or in the middle, for example Ferrari or Lamborghini, because of weight distribution.
So, that's enough about the engine for the moment – let's move on to the next stage …

UNIT 4, EXERCISE 6

🌀 16 **Speaker 1**
Where's the windscreen washer container?

🌀 17 **Speaker 2**
Do I have to wear protective clothing when I work on the battery?

🌀 18 **Speaker 3**
Do I have to change the coolant in the cooling system?

🌀 19 **Speaker 4**
How do I check how much brake fluid I have?

🌀 20 **Speaker 5**
Do I have to go to a service station to change my brake fluid?

🌀 21 **Speaker 6**
How often do I need to check the oil level?

🌀 22 **Speaker 7**
Do I need to do anything with the battery?

UNIT 4, EXERCISE 7

🌀 23

Rep	Can I help you?
Visitor	Oh, I was just looking at this model. It's really beautiful.
Rep	Yes, it certainly is. If design is important for you, then this is your car.
Visitor	Well, I do like nice design, but I'm also interested in the engine. How big is it?
Rep	It's a 4.2 litre V8 engine. With this new model, we have increased the power by 20 bhp to 330 bhp. And a six-speed automatic gearbox comes as standard.
Visitor	Right. So what's the top speed?
Rep	The top speed is 155 mph and it has an acceleration from 0 – 60 in only 6 seconds.
Visitor	Wow, that's impressive. Are there other engines available, or just the V8?
Rep	We're launching the model with a 3.7 and 4.2 litre petrol engine. A massive W12 and a smaller V6 will come later in the year.
Visitor	Uh huh. And what about fuel consumption?
Rep	Well, the car is made of aluminium which makes it the lightest in its class. That naturally has an effect on fuel consumption. The official government test figures say 16.1 mpg around town, with a combined best of just over 23 mpg for everyday motoring.
Visitor	Not bad. And how much does it cost?
Rep	This 4.2 model costs around £54,000. Included in the price is a six-disc CD unit with nine speakers, 18 inch alloy wheels and parking sensors.
Visitor	I must say it sounds very interesting. Do you have a brochure I could take with me?
Rep	Yes, of course. Here you are. Oh, and let me give you my card. If you have any other questions, then just call or email me. I'll be happy to help.
Visitor	I'll do that. Thanks very much for your time.

Rep   You're very welcome. Enjoy the rest of the show.

UNIT 5, EXERCISE 1

24

Journalist   So, you're finally ready to launch the successor to the popular XPT sedan.

Spokesperson   Yes, and I think you'll find that it was worth waiting for. We have optimized the car in several ways.

Journalist   I noticed. For example, when I drove the car before the press conference I felt some changes in the handling.

Spokesperson   That's right. The front suspension has been stiffened to produce more precise steering at high speeds. We have also increased the size of the disc brakes for a shorter braking distance.

Journalist   Right. Now, I also noticed that the press release says that there is improved fuel consumption. I'm surprised, as this is a more powerful, sporty car.

Spokesperson   Let me explain how we did it. Firstly, we have enhanced the Cd value with a new design. We have also reduced the kerb weight of the car by over 50 kilos by using light-weight materials. Actually, the big saving is in the urban consumption. We have introduced a start-stop automatic so that the engine cuts out if you stand still for more than three seconds and starts again when you take your foot off the brake. Ideal for the town. This has a positive effect on the running costs of this car and, of course, on the resale value.

Journalist   I see. Can I ask you about the interior? It definitely appears more spacious.

Spokesperson   It is. We have also increased the boot capacity to make the car more practical for families and sports people.

Journalist   Right. Well, I can see you've made a lot of interesting changes. I'll be sure to mention them in my article.

Spokesperson   Great. I look forward to reading it.

UNIT 5, EXERCISE 6

25

A   I need the dimensions of the new model, have you got them?

B   Of course, what do you need to know?

A   How long is the car body?

B   It's 4993 millimetres long, and 1857 millimetres wide.

A   What about the wheel base?

B   The wheel base is 2885 millimetres.

A   What is the height of the boot?

B   The boot height is approximately 690 millimetres, and the height of the car is 1398 millimetres.

A   What about the front and rear overhang?

B   The front and rear overhang? I'm not sure. Let me check the specifications ...

UNIT 5, EXERCISE 7

26

The average car is made up of a large number of different materials, as this pie chart here shows. Steel makes up by far the single largest percentage of materials, accounting for 55% of the car materials by weight. Then comes iron, with 13%. Plastics make up 10% of the car, although this percentage is naturally increasing all the time as car makers try to make vehicles lighter.

Aluminium accounts for 5% of the materials, although some cars contain much more. Some manufacturers are switching from steel to aluminium to save weight, because aluminium's so light. And new alloys mean that aluminium is now about as rigid as steel. Another advantage is that it's corrosion-resistant. It's going to be interesting to see if the popularity of aluminium continues to increase in the future.

Returning to my chart, you can see that rubber accounts for about 5% of the weight, and fluids and lubricants make up 4%. Zinc, lead and copper together account for 3%, and glass makes up 2%. All the other materials, including things like fabrics and ceramics, make up the final 3% together.

Now I'm going to move on to look at how the different materials can be recycled ....

UNIT 6, EXERCISE 1

27

Good morning everyone. For those of you who don't know me, my name is Gordon Waters. I'm here today to talk about NCAP – that's the New Car Assessment Programme. First of all, I'm going to tell you something about the history of the NCAP. Then I'll talk about the NCAP's passive vehicle safety programme. There'll be time for questions at the end. So, firstly, lets look at the NCAP's history. The NCAP was founded in 1997 and ... (FADE OUT)

(FADE IN) ... and that brings me on to my next point – the passive vehicle safety programme. This programme has set new standards for passive vehicle safety in Europe and America. Its aim is to provide the customer with an opportunity to compare passive vehicle safety in different car models. Just so that everyone's clear about the terminology, when I say passive vehicle safety, I mean those features used if an accident happens. Features which are used to avoid an accident are referred to as active vehicle safety. One important feature of the programme is ...(FADE OUT)

(FADE IN)...now we come to the tests themselves. As you can see in this slide, the programme first tested vehicles in a head-on collision with a rigid wall at 64 km/h. in this side-on crash, a 1.5 m wide deformable barrier weighing 950 kg is rammed into the side of the car at 50 km/h. A vehicle can be awarded up to five stars, depending on how it performs in the tests.

This next slide shows the four dummies which are used inside the car in the test. The driver and front passenger dummies not only measure the usual injury criteria, such as head, thorax, pelvic acceleration, and thigh pressure, but also neck pressure, thorax deformation, knee displacement, and lower leg pressure. At the rear are two smaller dummies in children's seats. A further test assesses the injury risk for pedestrians. OK, I think that covers everything about the tests. Now I'd just like to sum up by repeating my main points ...(FADE OUT)

UNIT 6, EXERCISE 1

Speaker 1
28 Excuse me, but did you say that the NCAP tests active and passive vehicle safety?

Speaker 2
29 Who does the NCAP provide information for, exactly?

Speaker 3
30 What did you say the crash speed in the frontal crash is?

Speaker 4
31 Did you say tested vehicles are given a percentage rating?

Speaker 5
32 Am I right in thinking the tests assess the risk of injury to the whole body?

Speaker 6
33 So these tests only assess the risk of injury to passengers, is that right?

UNIT 7, EXERCISE 4

34 We'll start by taking you through the stages of the design process. There are five phases, which take about three years in total.

First of all, product planning, marketing, and design come together. Product planning asks 'What could it be?', marketing asks 'Who is it for?' and design asks 'What does it look like?' I should maybe mention at this point that many cars are not really new, but are successors to, or derivatives of, existing models. The design of earlier models naturally needs to be taken into account.

Secondly, we have the concept phase where even more people are involved. We need to know what technology will be developed or adapted, which production plant and production processes are necessary and, finally, financial details such as volume and production costs.

In the concept phase we also produce a clay model, which has a ratio of 1:4. If it is approved, a 1:1 model is made and presented to a concept clinic. If there are no knock-out factors, the concept goes to a product clinic so that marketing factors can be finalized.

After the concept phase comes series development. The final design is specified. Several prototypes are handmade and tested in various climatic conditions and on different road surfaces.

After that is the pre-series phase where the production process and components from suppliers are tried out. A final marketing clinic is carried out to confirm price and market positioning. Then, if everything runs smoothly, there is a design and change freeze. The final phase is series production.

UNIT 8, EXERCISE 6

Eleonora Gentile
35 Let's now turn to new market opportunities. As you can see from the statistics here, the next big market is without doubt China. The level of car ownership is expected to rise to 50 million by the end of this decade. I'm absolutely certain that we need to expand operations in China now to meet this demand. There's a good chance of forming a joint venture with the China Motor Company, and this is what I would like to look at in more detail. First of all, I'm going to show you a breakdown of the costs involved ....

Uwe Schmidt
36 Let's move on to the next slide. We are convinced there's a good chance that we can increase sales by including swivelling headlights as standard equipment. The solid line represents sales with the headlights as standard. The dotted line indicates sales without, and the blue-coloured line shows potential sales with the lights as an optional extra. As you can see, offering the headlights as standard is clearly the best option. That's why we think it's highly probable that our main competitors will also follow this strategy.

Pascal Callabat
37 So, that brings me to the end of my talk today. It's possible that you do not agree with all the points of view I presented today about the intelligent car of the future. You may feel afraid of the new technology and the fact that the car will make all the decisions that drivers now make. Let me conclude by saying there's no doubt that the future means the end of driver self-determination in favour of the thinking car. Now, I'm sure you have some questions.

Cathy Epson
38 Hello. My name's Cathy Epson from Elite Satellite. I'm here today to talk to you abut the most significant development in driver comfort in the last ten years – telematics. I admit telematics has been slow to catch on, but we're convinced that will change in the near future as a result of our new package. We are offering voice-activated navigation, constant traffic monitoring, and, of course, SOS assistance. I'd like you to sit back and relax while I show you a short film which shows the benefits of our product.

Useful phrases and vocabulary

Asking for opinions

What do you think?
How do you feel about this?
What's your opinion of ... ?

Giving your opinion

I think ...
In my opinion ...
If you ask me ...

Agreeing and disagreeing

I agree.
I think so too.
Yes, that's right.

I'm afraid I don't agree.
No, sorry, I disagree.
I can't go along with that.

Recommending

I recommend ...
You need a car which ...
Have you thought about ... ?
Why don't you buy a ... ?
If I were you, I would buy a ...
A ... would be ideal/perfect for you.
You should/shouldn't buy a ...

Suggestions

Making suggestions
Why don't we ... ?
How about ... ?
I suggest ...
We could ...

Accepting suggestions
That sounds good.
I think that'll work.
Good idea.

Rejecting suggestions
I don't think that will work.
That's (maybe) not (such) a good idea because ...
I'm not sure about that.

Talking about advantages and disadvantages

One great advantage is ...
I think the ... feature is a big plus point.
One point in favour of the ... is ...
A major drawback/disadvantage is ...
I can see problems with the ...
The downside is ...

Describing a process

Firstly/The first step is/To begin with ...
Secondly ...
The next step/stage is ...
After that ...
Then ...
Following that ...
Finally ...
The last step/stage is ...

Talking about dimensions

How high/long/wide is the car/body/... ?
– It's ... millimetres long/high ...
What is the height/length/width of the boot/rear
    overhang/... ?
– The height/width is ... millimetres ...

Approximating

It's about/approximately/roughly ...
It must be at least ...
I think it's ...
I would guess it's ...
I don't know exactly but ...

Describing position

The ... is on the right/left-hand side of the engine.
This part is located at the front/rear of the engine.
It's on the opposite side of the engine from the ...
It's above/below/next to/beside the ...
It's between the ... and the ...

Describing shape

This layout is **cubical** in shape.
The brake fluid reservoir is the **rectangular**
    container on the right.

	noun	adjective
◯	circle	circular
⬤	sphere	spherical
▢	square	square
⬜	cube	cubical
▭	rectangle	rectangular
△	triangle	triangular
◁	cone	conical
⬭	cylinder	cylindrical

Talking about the future

Expressing certainty
I'm sure …
There's no doubt …
Without doubt …
I'm absolutely certain.

Expressing probability
There's a good chance …
It is quite likely …
It's probable …

Expressing possibility
It might happen.
It could well happen.
There's a possibility.

Making small talk

Introducing a topic
One car I really like is the …
I think one of the nicest/most attractive cars on the
  market is …
I saw a TV programme/read an article about …
  recently.
Someone told me the other day that …

Keeping the conversation going
What do you think of the … ?
Have you seen the … ?
It's really great/nice/beautiful/ugly, isn't it?
They must be fun to drive, don't you think?

Changing topic
By the way, …
Anyway, …
That reminds me of …
Speaking of …

Telephoning phrases

This is … from …
I'm calling about …
Can I speak to …, please?
Could you tell me the name of your company?
Could you repeat that, please?
I'm sorry, I didn't catch that.
I'll call you back later.
I'll send you … by fax/email.
Just give me a call if you have any more problems.
I'll get back to you as soon as I can.
Thanks for calling.

Making a presentation

Introducing yourself and your talk
For those of you who don't know me, my name is …
I'm here today to talk about/tell you something
  about …
I'm going to be speaking about …
Feel free to ask questions as we go along.
There'll be time for questions at the end.

Structuring the presentation
Firstly/Secondly/Thirdly/Finally …
Let's now look at …
Moving on, I'd like to say something about …
Now we come to …
That brings me on to my next point.
I think that covers everything about …

Referring to visuals
As you can see in this slide, …
This (next) slide shows …

Concluding
To sum up …
In conclusion …
I'd just like to repeat my main points.
Are there any questions?

Meeting phrases

Interrupting
Excuse me.
Could I come in here for a moment?
Sorry, can I say something?
I'd like to add something here.

Dealing with interruptions
Hang on a moment.
Can I just finish what I was saying?
We'll come to that point in a moment.
Let me just say one more thing.

At a trade fair

Visitor
I'd like more information on …
I'm interested in …
What about … ?
Can I take one of these brochures?
Could you tell me something about … ?

Sales rep
Can I help you?
Which car are you interested in?
Would you like more detailed information?
Would you like a brochure?
Here is our price list.
Let me give you my (business) card.

Email phrases

Thank you for your email.
I'm writing to …
I'm very sorry about …
Could you … ?
I'm sending you … as an attachment
I hope that …
Let me know if …
I look forward to hearing from you.
Best regards/Best wishes

British English	American English	Abbreviations	
accelerator	(also) gas pedal	ABC	Active Body Control
aerial	antenna	ABS	anti-lock (braking) system
aluminium	aluminum	ACC	automatic climate control
bonnet	hood	ASR	anti-spin regulation
boot	trunk	bhp	brake horsepower
camper van	recreational vehicle (RV)	CATS	Computer Active Technology Suspension
crossing	intersection	cc	cubic centimetre
driving licence	driver's license	Cd value	drag coefficient
engine	(also) motor	CDI	common-rail direct injection
estate car	station wagon	CI	compression ignition
gear lever/stick	gear shift/stick shift	cyl	cylinder
gearbox	transmission	ESP	electronic stability programme
glove compartment	(also) glove box	FWD	front-wheel drive
gudgeon pin	piston pin	GDI	gasoline direct injection
indicator	turn signal	GPS	global positioning system
kerb weight	curb weight	ind	independent
lorry	truck	kph	kilometres per hour
motorway	highway, freeway	kW	kilowatt
number plate	license plate	LHD	left-hand drive
oil sump	oil pan	mpg	miles per gallon
MPV	(also) minivan	mph	miles per hour
people carrier	MPV or minivan	MPV	multi-purpose vehicle
petrol cap/flap	gas tank lid	MY	model year
petrol station	gas station	n/a	not applicable
petrol tank	gas tank	Nm	Newton metre
roundabout	traffic circle	pb	power brakes
saloon	sedan	ps	power steering
side light	parking light	pw	power windows
silencer	muffler	RHD	right-hand drive
subway	underpass	rpm	revolutions per minute
swept volume	piston displacement	RV	recreational vehicle
tyre	tire	RWD	rear-wheel drive
windscreen	windshield	SI	spark ignition
wing mirror	side mirror	SUV	sport utility vehicle
wing	fender	TDI	turbo direct injection
		ZEV	zero-emission vehicle

Useful verbs (in context)

to accelerate	The car accelerates from 0–60mph in 6 seconds.
to accommodate	The car accommodates five people comfortably.
to adjust	The steering wheel can be adjusted to suit you.
to brake	He braked just in time to avoid the dog.
to consume	The car consumes more fuel in town.
to equip	The car is equipped with eight airbags.
to fail	We couldn't stop because the brakes failed.
to fit	We have fitted new tyres.
to ignite	A spark plug ignites the mixture.
to inject	Fuel is injected directly into the combustion chamber.
to launch	We are launching the car next month.
to lubricate	Oil lubricates the moving parts.
to overtake	Don't overtake going up a hill.
to press	If you press this switch, the sliding roof opens.
to recall	The cars were recalled because of a defect.
to rotate	The motion of the piston rotates the crankshaft.
to tow	They towed the car to the nearest petrol station.
to weigh	The car weighs about 2 tonnes.

Weights and measures conversion chart

	NON-METRIC		METRIC
weight (UK)		= 1 ounce (oz)	= 28.35 grams (g)
	16 ounces	= 1 pound (lb)	= 0.454 kilogram (kg)
	14 pounds	= 1 stone (st)	= 6.356 kilograms
	8 stone	= 1 hundredweight (cwt)	= 50.8 kilograms
	20 cwt	= 1 (long) ton	= 1016.04 kilograms
		1 tonne (t)	= 1000 kilograms
weight (US)		1 ounce (oz)	= 28.35 grams (g)
	16 ounces	= 1 pound (lb)	= 0.454 kilogram (kg)
	100 pounds	= 1 hundredweight (cwt)	= 45.359 kilograms
	20 cwt	= 1 (short) ton (t)	= 907.18 kilograms
length		1 inch (1 in; 1'')	= 25.4 millimetres (mm)
	12 inches	= 1 foot (1 ft; 1')	= 30.48 centimetres (cm)
	3 feet	= 1 yard (yd)	= 0.914 metre (m)
	1760 yards	= 1 mile (m)	= 1.609 kilometres (km)
surface		1 square inch (sq in)	= 6.452 sq centimetres (cm^2)
	144 sq inches	= 1 sq foot (sq ft)	= 929.03 cm^2
	9 sq feet	= 1 sq yard (sq yd)	= 0.836 sq metre (m^2)
	4840 sq yards	= 1 acre	= 0.405 hectare (ha)
	640 acres	= 1 sq mile (sq m)	= 2.59 km^2
volume		1 cubic inch (cu in)	= 16.4 cm^3 or cc
	1728 cubic inches	= 1 cubic foot (cu ft)	= 0.028 m^3
	27 cubic feet	= 1 cubic yard (cu yd)	= 0.765 m^3
capacity (UK)	20 fluid ounces (fl oz)	= 1 pint (pt)	= 0.568 litre (l)
	2 pints	= 1 quart (qt)	= 1.136 litres
	4 quarts	= 1 gallon (gal)	= 4.546 litres
capacity (US)	16 fluid ounces (fl oz)	= 1 pint (pt)	= 0.473 liter (l)
	2 pints	= 1 quart (qt)	= 0.946 liters
	4 quarts	= 1 gallon (gal)	= 3.785 liters